John

Happy Cooking

I want you to try some of the spices, I think you will like it.

Mclass Dichdu

JJ,

EIGHTEEN YEARS OF GREAT FOOD & FRIENDS AND LOTS MORE TO COME! THANKS SO MUCH FOR YOUR FRIENDSHIP & SUPPORT. KITCHENIQUE'S BEEN QUITE A JOURNEY & YOU'VE MADE IT SO SPECIAL FOR SO MANY OF US!

LOVE,
Vicki

Saffron to Sassafras

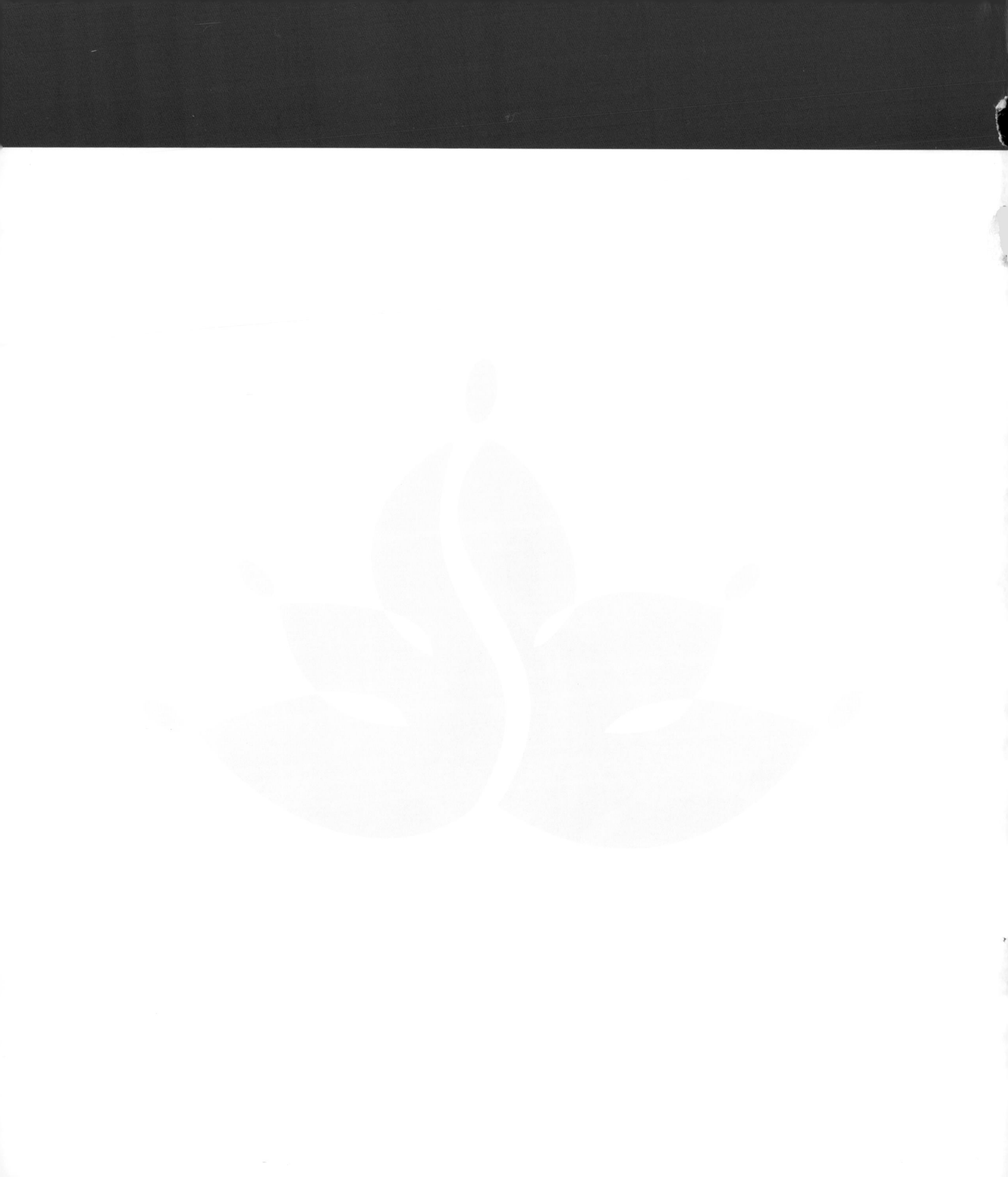

Saffron to Sassafras

Presented by:
"Sharing Shores"
Indian Women's Association, Inc.

Sharing Shores

Saffron to Sassafras

ISBN number: 0-9771584-0-3

Edited, Designed and Printed by
Graphic Point Pvt. Ltd.
4th Floor, Harbans Bhawan II
Nangal Rai Commercial Complex
New Delhi 110 046 (India)
Telefax: 91-11-28523517, 28523112
Email: gppl@graphicpointindia.com

Design Pooja Sharma, Ravi Raj

Editor Anil Mehrotra

Photography Jay Patel

All proceeds from the sale of Saffron to Sassafras will benefit
the community and the women and children charities.

First Edition 5000 copies

Contents

Sharing Shores, Indian Women's Organization, Inc.

Mission Statement

"Sharing Shores" is a non- profit volunteer organization of women of Indian origin committed to preservation, promotion, and sharing of the rich culture and culinary heritage of India. It is dedicated to improving the lives and welfare of underprivileged women and children of the local community. Funds raised will be used for supporting these efforts.

Board of Directors

Anita Jhunjunwala

Bhavna Desai

Chandan Sharma

Krishna Agnihotri

Pinki Diwan

Meena Sachdev

Sumir Chehl

Baton Rouge has a fairly significant enclave of people with an Indian heritage that sprouted about twenty years earlier, principally as a result of strong foreign students recruitment programs at local universities. In 1980, the city of Baton Rouge, Louisiana hosted the World Hindu Conference, an event that brought more than ten thousand people with ties to India to one venue downtown. These people included citizens from India, U.S. residents with Indian heritage, world leaders, as well as State and local officials from Louisiana. I was then twelve years old and attended the event with my parents as part of the host community.

What I remember about the World Hindu Conference was not the speeches, singing or dancing; and there certainly was a lot of that. What I do remember however, was the preparation of the food. As a child living in a very integrated, academic community, my parents would often make both "Indian" and "American" food. I usually preferred American food, in part because it's what all the other kids were eating, but also because, lets face it, an aloo parantha would never truly be a good substitute for a chili cheese dog at the ballpark.

For the conference, all of the local aunties got together for weeks in advance to prepare for the event. These "professional" ladies prepared huge amounts of food (by hand, for hours at a time), to serve to the masses.

This included dishes we loved and were stewed, baked, rolled and stuffed in vats, basins, and containers of epic proportions. There were thousands of gulab jamuns bobbing in sugar sauce, even more glazed jalebees, and literally hundreds of pounds of "burfees". It was only years later, that I could fully appreciate their decision to do it all themselves. In fact, I don't think any other alternative ever crossed their minds.

The book you are holding is a book of recipes from this very community. It includes the recipes of many of those same aunties who cooked those traditional foods twenty five years ago, and who still cook those foods, albeit in much smaller proportions, every day across South Louisiana.

But the food has changed, just as its authors and cooks have changed. Certain variations in the book are intended to pick up regional ingredients and adopt local flavors. Cousequently, this natural fusion of Indian Creole, and Cajun foods has resulted in some new local recipes that can now be shared outside of South Louisiana.

The natural fusion reflected in many of these recipes also parallels broader changes in our community as it has grown and further integrated locally. While the principal authors were Indian-born immigrants to America, their principal diners, however, are mostly American-born and these recipes are not generation specific. Frankly, no matter how hard we might try to recreate the food of our childhood, we wouldn't be able to. It wouldn't taste quite the same, the making of it wouldn't sound quite the same, and the food itself wouldn't be the same. That's the problem with so many people's understanding of these foods. Everyone wants to know if it's "authentic", which naturally requires a comparison. With the popularity of Indian and fusion cuisine in America continuing to rise, and as more generations of Indians are established here, such comparisons are becoming increasingly meaningless or irrelevant. And, in my view, that is as it should be.

The recipes contained in this book reflect a community of Indian heritage that has matured in South Louisiana and has integrated itself into the American way of life. While not always easy, this fusion in food, as in life, is a tribute to all the aunties- constituting the very foundation of that community. That they wanted to prepare this book and share it with others should not come as a surprise to anyone. In fact, just as they have for almost forty years, they wouldn't have had it any other way, nor would they have taken no for an answer.

By Amit Sachdev

Introduction

In the era of cookbooks galore, who would dare to challenge the finger-flick availability of recipes on the internet or try to compete with the ever-growing cookbook accessibility in the bookstores and libraries. However, "Sharing Shores," claims that "Saffron to Sassafras" is one of a kind cookbook, unique in several ways. It is an Indian community cookbook, which in itself is rare. The book is an expression of a deep passion felt by the women of the "Sharing-Shores", longing to leave a legacy of their fascinating journey from their motherland to the adopted homeland and a desire to preserve, promote and share their rich culinary heritage with their new community, their children and the generations to come. The contributors, therefore, have shared their most prized recipes, the culinary secrets and cherished memories of their path. The proceeds from this book will benefit the needs of underprivileged women and children of the local community.

"Saffron to Sassafras" offers a precious collection of culturally diverse culinary customs and traditions from India. In addition, it also presents a wealth of adaptations of technology, techniques and modern facilities in order to keep in step with the racing pace of the present-day life style. The book includes a feast for all palates, vegetarians, non-vegetarians, the pros and the novices. "Saffron to Sassafras" includes anecdotal and original stories from personal experiences of the contributors and not from historic or cyber sources.

The women of "Sharing Shores" affectionately share their knowledge of the time-honored culinary skills and techniques learnt from the kitchens of their mothers and grandmothers in different parts of India. It uses ingredients that are readily available in the American supermarkets or from the specialty stores. The adaptation of the Indian cuisine with the exciting Cajun and Creole cuisines of Louisiana, using a blend of the traditional and non-traditional ingredients and techniques, presents a delicious merger of tastes. The book also contains a section on fusion cookery. Although many recipes have been modified to make them simple, quick and easy, the authenticity of the taste and the appearance of the dishes has been preserved.

With the ever-growing popularity of Indian foods and the mushrooming of Indian restaurants of all grades and tastes in every place, the enthusiasm for home cooking is, however, on the wane. The guests are often entertained at the restaurants for convenience of time and effort. "Saffron to Sassafras," replete with a simplified approach to the art of Indian cooking, offers to change all that. It is geared for assurance of success for our children to reproduce the taste and aroma of Mom's cooking. It is meant to encourage all those friends who have refrained from Indian cooking at home due to involved methodology, to once again, bring the charm and the warmth of the Indian hospitality, and the pleasures of Indian dining to their tables at home and to honor their guests with full fervor of the loving, welcoming and glamorous traditions of the Indian continuum.

The Upanishads-ancient philosophical treatise from the Vedas-say,
"O householder of little sense,
Leave your guest at home
With no food,
All your merits
Earned from good company
And pleasant conversation,
Your offerings and prayers to the deities,
Your hopes and expectations
Then come to nothing."
-Upanishads

Translated by Poree Sengupta

According to the dictates of Indian hospitality, every guest is to be treated as an honored person and every visitor is to be offered food and drink upon arrival. The visitors are often insisted to stay on for a meal. "Saffron to Sassafras," offers, not just recipes, but also love and wisdom of those who have used them to nourish and nurture their families and friends. We hope that cooking from "Saffron to Sassafras" will be exciting and provide a memorable culinary experience.

By Sumir Chehl

"The diversity of our community is such a great part of our society - especially when it takes the form of an exceptional cookbook like Saffron to Sassafras by Sharing Shores. The cookbook allows us to share the rich culture of our city and the talent of an organization dedicated to improving the quality of life of our citizens."

Mayor-President Melvin L. "Kip" Holden

"Shortly after I began my journey three years ago as the Executive Director for the Battered Women's Program, I met a charming, talented delegation of women. These women, who became Sharing Shores, wanted to create a cookbook to help raise funds for the Battered Women's Program. During each of our meetings I was impressed with their dedication to this effort, the creativity of the individuals and the group, and the wonderful opportunity to reach across geography, culture, and time, in order to help develop a more caring community. We support Sharing Shores community cookbook "Saffron to Sassafras". It creates family time in the kitchen while deliciously introducing an ancient and graceful culture. On behalf of the Battered Women's Program, I thank Sharing Shores for their commitment to support our mission, and for their willingness to share their time, their talents, their wisdom – and their wonderful, mouthwatering recipes!"

Martha G. Forbes, M.P.A., LCSW
Executive Director
Battered Women's Program

"Louisiana is a State with a rich diverse culture, always open to authentic culinary experiences. Creatively spiced dishes in India are delicious, and resemble the indigenous cuisine found here. I am thrilled to support Sharing Shores Indian food cookbook Saffron to Sassafras! These ladies have been helping the local community in introducing the fascinating culinary traditions of Indian culture and cuisine, and we're so glad to have them."

Susan Strange Tugwell
Owner, Unique Cuisine Catering

Hummus

Snacks and Appetizers

Aloo Dal Vada *(Potato Lentil Fritters)*

1 pound red potatoes, boiled, peeled and grated
1 cup chana dal
2-3 serrano peppers, finely chopped
1- inch piece of ginger, peeled and grated
½ cup minced onion
2 teaspoons salt
½ teaspoon cumin seeds
½ teaspoon cayenne pepper
1 tablespoon lemon juice
Oil for frying

Soak chana dal in 2 cups of water for 1 hour. Drain and remove 2 tablespoons of dal to a small bowl. Grind the rest of dal using a food processor. You can also chop peppers and ginger in the food processor. Mix potatoes with all the ingredients including saved dal. Make 1-inch balls, flatten to a 2-inch disk and make a hole in the center. This is called a vada. Make vadas with remaining balls. Heat vegetable oil in a deep pan and fry the vadas on high heat. Drain on paper towels and serve with cilantro chutney.

Variation

Aloo Poha Vada

Instead of dal, use 1 cup of poha (pressed rice). Soak poha in water for 10 minutes, rinse and use. Adding ¼ cup of chopped cilantro improves the flavor.

Chicken Tikka

2 pounds skinless, boneless chicken breast, cut in 1-inch pieces

Marinade
2 tablespoons white vinegar
2 tablespoons grated ginger
1 teaspoon granulated garlic powder
1 teaspoon cayenne pepper
½ to 1 teaspoon garam masala
2 teaspoons coriander powder
1 teaspoon cumin seeds, roasted and powdered
2 teaspoons salt
½ teaspoon turmeric
2-3 drops red food color
2 tablespoons oil

Garnish
1 medium onion, sliced
2 tablespoons fresh cilantro, chopped
Lemon slices

Wash chicken and pat dry. In a large glass or steel bowl, mix all marinade ingredients. Add chicken and marinate at least 2 hours or up to 24 hrs in the refrigerator. Preheat oven to 350°F. Skewer chicken on oiled skewers. Lay skewers on a roasting rack. Cook for 10 to15 minutes. Turn over, baste with marinade and cook for 10 minutes more. Check meat for doneness by piercing with a fork. The juices should not run pink. Serve over dry sautéed sliced onions, sprinkle with fresh chopped cilantro and garnish with slices of lemon. Can also be served on a bed of salad greens, topped with cilantro vinaigrette, green onion flowers, and lemon slices. Alternatively, serve with marinated sliced onions in fresh lemon juice, salt and cilantro chutney Serves 6.

Nawabi Chicken Tikka

These nawabi (royal) creamy white morsels of chicken just melt in your mouth; the spices used here, help to retain the white color.

2¼ pounds skinless boneless chicken breast
½ cup sour cream
½ cup thick plain yogurt
4 tablespoons malt or white vinegar
3 serrano chilies, seeded and ground to a paste
1 tablespoon fresh ginger paste
1 tablespoon fresh garlic paste
1 tablespoon vegetable oil
2 teaspoons salt
1 teaspoon white pepper powder
½ teaspoon mace

Wash and dry chicken on paper towels. Cut chicken into 1 to 1 ½ inch cubes, about 30-36 pieces. In a non-reactive bowl, mix rest of ingredients together and marinate the chicken in the yogurt mixture for 2 to 3 hours in the refrigerator or overnight.

Preheat oven to 350°F. Place chicken on skewers or on a broiling pan; keep a tray underneath to catch the drippings. Bake for 15 minutes. Baste with remaining marinade, then turn over and baste the other side. Bake for another 7-10 minutes.

Do not over-bake, as chicken will dry out. Time taken to cook will depend on the brand of chicken and how long it has been marinated.

Seekh Kabab

1 pound boneless leg of lamb or goat
1 teaspoon ginger/garlic paste
2 teaspoons chopped hot green chili pepper
1 cup cilantro with stems, finely chopped
1 onion, finely chopped and squeezed to remove water
½ cup bread crumbs
2 teaspoons garam masala
1 teaspoon cumin powder
½ teaspoon cayenne pepper
1 tablespoon lemon juice
Salt to taste
Skewers to make kababs
Vegetable oil for basting

Cut meat into small pieces, wash and remove excess water, dry on paper towels

Mix all the ingredients except oil in a food processor, grind to a coarse paste. Keep aside in refrigerator until you are ready to make kababs. Knead the mix well and divide into small balls (16-20). Using wet hands roll the meat on a skewer to get ½ inch diameter sausage like rolls. Cook on a hot grill or in an oven, preheated to 350 °F. After 5 minutes, baste with oil, turn, baste again and cook until done (about 10 minutes). Serve with mint chutney and sliced onions. Preparation time 30 minutes. Cooking time 15 minutes. Serves 4.

Goat meat is available only in a few Indian grocery stores. Apply a little oil to the grill to prevent the meat from sticking.

Turkey Kabab

2 pounds ground turkey
1 ½ teaspoons salt
½ onion, chopped
5 cloves garlic, chopped fine, about 4 teaspoons
2 tablespoons cilantro, finely chopped
1 tablespoon fresh ginger, chopped or shredded
1 teaspoon garam masala
1 teaspoon tandoori masala (Rajah Brand preferred)
Fresh breadcrumbs, made from 4 slices of bread
1 teaspoon coriander powder
1 tablespoon hot green pepper, chopped
1 egg
1 tablespoon oil or butter
Skewers
Roasted red or green bell peppers and / or green onions, chopped (optional)

Preheat oven to 450°F. Spray a roasting pan with Pam or line with foil.

Mix all ingredients together except butter. Add optional ingredients and mix. Divide the mixture into 7 portions. Take a gallon size Ziploc bag or a thick sheet of plastic. Take one portion of meat and spread it flat on the plastic (6 inches long x 4 inches wide x 1inch thick). Place a skewer along the wide side of the meat and roll the meat on the skewer in jellyroll fashion. Place the roll on the prepared roasting pan. Make meat rolls with the remaining meat. Cook meat for 15 minutes. Using tongs, turn the meat over and lower the temperature to 400°F. Cook for another 15 minutes. When cooked, brush with melted butter and wrap in foil. After 5 minutes, remove the skewers. Slice the kababs diagonally, in 2-inch pieces. Alternatively, the rolls can be grilled outdoors. Do not overcook. Serve with tamarind sauce. Makes 21 pieces.

Serving suggestion: Heat a nonstick griddle. Spray with non-stick spray. Add chunks of onions and bell pepper. On this bed of onions, lay the kababs and provide toothpicks for picking up the kababs.

Handwa

Handwa is a specialty of Gujarat. It can be eaten as a whole food or as a snack item. It goes very well with a nice pickle or a hot cup of tea. This delight is high in protein.

1 ½ cups coarsely ground rice
½ cup coarsely ground chana dal
Or use 2 cups handwa flour
1 ½ cups yogurt
2-3 cloves garlic
1 ½ -inch piece of ginger
2 serrano peppers
1 medium onion, shredded
1 zucchini, shredded
3 teaspoons salt
¾ teaspoon turmeric
¼ teaspoon cayenne pepper
½ teaspoon garam masala
2 tablespoons cilantro, chopped
½ teaspoon baking soda
1 tablespoon lemon juice
2 tablespoons oil
2 ½ teaspoons sesame seeds
¼ teaspoon mustard seeds
¼ teaspoon cumin seeds
1-inch stick cinnamon, broken into pieces
2 cloves
10-12 kari leaves

Mix ground rice and chana dal or handwa flour together in a large bowl. Add yogurt and enough water to make a thick cake-like batter. Leave covered, overnight, in a warm place to rise. Grind garlic, ginger and serrano pepper to a paste. Add to the batter along with grated onion, zucchini, salt, turmeric, cayenne, garam masala and chopped cilantro, and stir well. Lastly, add soda and lemon juice and mix well. Preheat oven to 400°F. In a 9x13-inch pan, heat oil, add sesame, mustard and cumin seeds, cinnamon, cloves and kari leaves. When the seeds begin to splutter, pour the batter in the pan. Bake for 25-35 minutes. Handwa is done when a toothpick inserted in the center comes out clean, and sides are brown. Broil 3-4 minutes to brown the top. Cut in squares and serve warm.

You can substitute cabbage, squash, spinach etc. for zucchini. Handwa flour is available at Indian stores. Adding baking soda and lemon juice just before baking makes handwa much lighter.

Khandvi *(Microwave Method)*

Khandvi is a popular appetizer from Gujarat. Making it takes a little practice. This recipe offers a quick and easy microwave method.

½ cup chickpea flour (besan)
½ cup plain sour yogurt
½ cup water
½ teaspoon green chili-ginger paste
¼ teaspoon turmeric
1 pinch asafetida
Salt to taste
2 tablespoons oil
1 teaspoon mustard seeds
3 tablespoons coconut, grated
2 tablespoons cilantro leaves, chopped

Mix chickpea flour, yogurt, water, chili-ginger paste, turmeric, asafetida and salt in a microwave–safe glass bowl to make a smooth batter. Microwave on high for 6 to 8 minutes, stirring every 1½ minutes. Using a flexible spatula spread the mixture on a lightly greased smooth surface as a thin layer (about 1/8-inch thick). Cool for 2 to 3 minutes. Make slits, 1½-inch apart along the width with a blunt knife or spatula. Carefully roll each strip like a jellyroll and place on a serving plate.

For Baghar

Heat oil in a small skillet over moderate heat. Add mustard seeds and asafetida. When they begin to splutter remove from heat and pour on top of the rolls. Garnish with grated coconut and chopped cilantro leaves.

Keep yogurt at room temperature for several hours to make it sour. Alternatively, add a few drops of lemon juice. It makes a subtle difference. Bottled green chili-ginger paste is available in Indian stores. It can also be made by grinding fresh ginger and hot green chilies with a mortar and pestle. A clean counter-top smeared with a thin film of oil works well to spread the khandvi paste.

Hummus

This very popular Middle Eastern appetizer has become a favorite with Indians as well as others in the USA. Garbanzo beans are widely used in the state of Punjab in India. They are a good source of protein for the vegetarians. This is an easy and healthy appetizer that even teens can make.

1 can (15 ounce) garbanzo beans (chickpeas)
2 tablespoons Tahini
2 teaspoons fresh lemon juice
¼ teaspoon salt
¼ teaspoon fresh minced garlic
Cayenne pepper, paprika or black olives for garnish optional
Pita bread

Rinse garbanzo beans and drain water. Put all the ingredients in a blender and blend until it becomes a paste. Pour in a flat serving dish. Garnish with paprika, cayenne pepper or black olives on top. Serve with warm pita bread.
Serves 4.

Tahini (sesame seed paste) is available in Indian or Middle Eastern grocery stores.

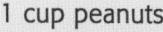

Masala Peanuts (Spicy Peanuts)

1 cup peanuts
2 to 3 tablespoons oil
1 ½ teaspoons salt
For Masala (Spice mixture)
2 teaspoons mango powder (amchur)
1 teaspoon garam masala
1 teaspoon coriander/cumin powder mixture
½ to 1 teaspoon cayenne pepper
½ teaspoon turmeric
½ teaspoon chaat masala
¼ to ½ teaspoon citric acid

Roast peanuts until the raw taste is gone. Remove the papery skin. Heat oil in a microwave safe dish on low 1 minute. Add peanuts and all the ingredients for the masala. Mix well and keep aside for 30 minutes so that the peanuts absorb the spiced oil. Store in an airtight container. Stays fresh for several days.

These spicy peanuts are often served with cocktails. Use raw Spanish peanuts found at farmers markets as they have a sweeter taste.

Muthia

1 cup cream of wheat
¾ cup whole-wheat flour
1 zucchini, shredded
1 small bunch spinach, chopped
½ - inch piece ginger, finely grated
2 cloves garlic, chopped
1 hot green chili pepper, chopped
1 teaspoon cumin seeds
1 ½ teaspoons coriander powder
½ teaspoon turmeric
1 ½ teaspoons cayenne pepper
3 teaspoons salt
2 tablespoons lemon juice
Water to bind
½ teaspoon baking soda
1 teaspoon lemon juice

For Baghaar
2 tablespoon oil
½ teaspoon mustard seed
½ teaspoon cumin seeds
1 teaspoon sesame seed

Mix cream of wheat and whole-wheat flour in a large bowl. Add zucchini, spinach, ginger, garlic, chili, cumin, coriander, turmeric, cayenne, salt, oil and lemon juice and enough water to make a soft dough. Sprinkle baking soda and lemon juice and knead some more. Shape dough in oblong sausage-like pieces and steam for 20-25 minutes. It is done when a toothpick inserted in the center, comes out clean.

To steam, simply place pieces on a pan sprayed with oil. Place on a rack in a 5-quart pot, which has about 2 inches of water. When cool; slice muthia in ¼ -inch pieces. In a large skillet heat oil and add mustard, cumin and sesame seeds. When the seeds begin to splutter, add muthia and stir gently until a little crisp.

Sprinkling baking soda and lemon juice at the very last, helps to make the dough light. Zucchini and spinach can be substituted with finely shredded cabbage, cucuzza or any left over rice, dal or vegetable. Flour can be substituted with chichpea flour (besan), corn flour or any coarse flour.

Quick Dhokla

1 cup chana dal
1 ½ hot green chili pepper or 1 ½ teaspoon chili paste
1-inch piece fresh ginger, peeled or 1 teaspoon ginger paste
2 teaspoons salt
3 tablespoons sugar
2 teaspoons oil
2 packages (1- teaspoon) Eno, divided
6 tablespoons lemon juice, divided

For Baghaar or Tadka for each pan

2 tablespoons oil
½ teaspoon cumin seeds
½ teaspoon mustard seeds
¼ teaspoon sesame seeds
1 eno package to each thali
Optional: grated coconut and chopped cilantro

Wash and soak chana dal for 1 ½ hours in at least 3 cups of water. Drain dal and grind to a fine paste with serrano pepper and ginger, adding gradually a small amount of water. Add salt, sugar, oil, and mix well, adding water, if necessary, to make a thick batter. Spray two 8-inch cake pans or thalis with oil. Pour batter equally in the pans. Just before steaming each pan, sprinkle Eno and lemon juice over the batter and mix. In a 5-quart pot bring to a boil 2 inches of water and steam the dhokla batter; 1 pan at a time for approximately 15 minutes. Insert a toothpick in the center, if the toothpick comes out clean, the dhokla is ready. Let dhokla cool a few minutes, cut into 1 ½ -inch squares and make baghaar. Heat oil in a small skillet. Add mustard seeds and cover when the seeds pop pour over the dhokla. Garnish with coconut and cilantro, if desired. Serve warm with cilantro chutney. Makes 2 pans.

Eno is available at Indian grocery stores. It is a leavening agent similar to baking powder.

Pakoras

This recipe was used for several fundraisers that were done to raise money for the publication of the cookbook. You can cut down the proportions and use the recipe for a much smaller party.

5 pounds potatoes, peeled and shredded
5 pounds onions, peeled and sliced
3 pounds zucchini, washed and shredded
1 pound hot peppers
1 pound fresh ginger, peeled
1 head cauliflower, cut into small pieces
4 (10 ounce) packets frozen spinach, thawed and drained
¾ cup salt
½ cup cumin seeds
½ cup garam masala
¼ cup mango powder (optional)
5 pounds chickpea flour (besan)
1 cup corn meal or cornflour
Oil for frying

Using a food processor, chop ginger and pepper. Change blade and shred or slice all vegetables except cauliflower. Place the vegetables in a very large mixing bowl. Add all other ingredients and mix well. Heat oil in a large wok to 350°F and using a tablespoon, drop the batter in hot oil. Fry until golden brown. May need to add more besan as the mixture continues to release water. Serve immediately or keep warm. Leftovers can be frozen and used as koftas in tomato onion gravy. Makes 500 pakoras.

Ragra Patties

Ragra

2 cups whole dried peas, soaked for
6-8 hours
6 to 8 cups water
1 teaspoon salt
Pinch of baking soda
1 medium onion chopped (1 cup)
2 tablespoons garlic, chopped
4 tablespoons oil
5 teaspoons lemon juice
3 teaspoons cayenne pepper powder
1 teaspoon turmeric
Chopped jalapenos to taste
3 tablespoons chickpea flour (besan)
1/3 cup water
1 - 1 1/2 teaspoons salt
3 teaspoons sugar

Pressure-cook the peas in 6 cups water, salt and baking soda until soft and a small amount of water remains. Alternatively, cook peas in 8 cups of water in a large saucepan over moderate heat until soft for about 40 minutes to 1 hour. Heat oil and fry onions until golden brown. Add garlic, cook until pale brown. Add lemon juice, pepper, turmeric and jalapeno peppers. Sauté for 30 seconds. Add 2 cups of water and 1 to 1½ teaspoons of salt. Make a paste with chickpea flour and 1/3 cup water. Add to the pea mix to thicken it. Add sugar. Stir and cook for 5 minutes to blend flavors. Serve hot.

Patties

6 medium potatoes, (about 2 pounds)
boiled, peeled and mashed
½ cup cornstarch
2 teaspoons salt

Mix all ingredients together. Roll out to ¼ inch thickness on a floured board. Cut into 2-inch circles. Pan sauté on both sides. Serve with Ragra and mithi (sweet) date chutney.

Variation to the patties: Add cooked peas or chopped cashews in the center of patti and seal it in the potatoes.

Chaat Times

21

"Let's go get Chaat"

Is a common cry of Indian teenagers and young adults whether they live in India or other big cities in the U.S., Canada or England. Chaat cafés are becoming a current trend similar to coffee houses. Others in smaller towns have to get it from ethnic restaurants or depend on mom to prepare their favorite kind of chaat. Popularity of such a delightful fun food is soaring, mostly due to availability of all ingredients and good recipes.

Chaat is not one recipe, it is more of a grouping of certain types of foods, served in a certain way and as with teatime in India, served with evening tea, or as a starter for a party or just a hearty snack in place of a meal. It has become a great gatherer for festivals, celebrations and other parties.

As with other foods, chaat can have regional influence and taste. In Mumbai, one eats Bhel with the savory chutneys. In Punjab, one finds Aloo Tikki with Chhole and Dahi Vada; in Uttar Pradesh, it is predominantly Kachories, and Samosa with tamarind chutney. In the South, one finds Dal Vada, and Idli with coconut chutney. Papri chaat and Gol Guppas, also known as Pani Puri, is universal throughout India.

Aloo Tikki *(Potato Discs)*

Aloo tikki can be made in several different ways. A simple one is made with just boiled potatoes, salt and a little cayenne powder. Others are stuffed with seasoned peas or chopped green beans. They can be eaten either with cilantro chutney, date chutney, or ketchup. When the tikki is not stuffed, it is often topped with spicy garbanzo beans (chhole) or spicy peas (ragra). Tikkis are usually pan fried on a cast iron griddle but deep frying is much faster.

4 medium potatoes, about 1 pound
5 slices bread
1 teaspoon salt
1 teaspoon garam masala
Pinch of black pepper

Boil the potatoes until they are soft. Peel and mash the potatoes. Process the bread in a food processor to make bread crumbs. Add to the potatoes. Add salt, garam masala and black pepper. Mix well. Make 1to 2-inch balls and flatten them into a thick disk or "tikki". Deep fry the tikkis in very hot oil on medium high heat. Drain on a paper towel. Serve hot with cilantro chutney. Serves 6 – 8.

Aloo Chhole

1 pound (2 cups) garbanzo beans (kabuli chhole)
2 quarts boiling water
3 teaspoons salt
3 pieces bay leaves
¼ teaspoon clove powder
¼ teaspoon cinnamon powder
½ teaspoon red hot pepper
½ teaspoon black pepper
1 teaspoons cumin seeds
1 tablespoon cumin powder
2 teaspoons paprika
1 teaspoons red hot pepper
1 tablespoon mango powder
1 tablespoon tamarind paste
½ cup hot water
¼ cup oil
1 teaspoon cumin seeds
1 large sliced onion
1 cubic inch fresh ginger, thinly sliced
3 large green chili peppers
2 teaspoons pomegranate seeds, finely ground
¼ cup cilantro
¼ cup sliced red onions soaked in 1 table spoon of lemon juice
4 thin wedges lemon
6-8 wedges tomato or ¼ cup chopped tomato
4 medium size red potatoes, each cut into 8 long wedges and deep fried.
1 ½ teaspoons salt for potatoes

Chhole-Bhature (plural bhatura), originally a Punjabi specialty, is now popular among all Indians. It is served with equal fervor as an any-time snack, a chaat item, a full meal at the Dhabas or street carts or at gourmet's gala. The way-side hawkers sell chhole on neighborhood corners, market places, parks, beaches and other gathering places and in front of the cinema halls all across India. A large, highly polished brass *Pateela** is staged on one of the two *Angeethies*** in the middle of a cart. A large flat *Tawa* (griddle) is set on the other angeethi to warm Bhature. Bhature are stacked 6-8 high in a semicircle around the pateela. Chhole-Bhature are served sizzling hot, topped with tamarind chatni, and diced raw onions, tomatoes, cilantro and hot green pepper. The vendor is often invisible behind the waiting crowd but the aroma draws people of all ages. It has now become a standard item on menus at the fast-food joints for added attraction.

Pateela: a pot with a constricted narrow neck, wide-girth with round convex bottom; the interior is nickel plated.

**Angeethi:* a portable charcoal stove made from a round tin can, about 1 foot in diameter and 10-14 inches high. The interior and exterior walls are thickly coated with potter's clay. Charcoal is set on a built-in grid. This homemade charcoal stove used to be the standard means of cooking prior to the advent of propane gas burners and electric stoves in India.

Wash beans thoroughly and soak in 2 quarts boiling water for four hours in a large bowl. Drain and rinse. Transfer chhole to a 6 quart pot. Add 2 quarts fresh water, salt, bay leaves, clove powder, cinnamon powder, hot pepper, black pepper and cumin seeds. Boil until chhole are very tender (1 to 1 ½ hours). Alternatively, pressure-cook for 15 minutes under 15 pounds pressure and let stand until the pressure drops completely. Decant the thick liquid and save for later use. Discard bay leaves.

Mix cumin powder, paprika, red hot pepper and mango powder and divide this dry spice mix into three equal portions.

Heat oil in a 6-quart cast-iron skillet or an iron wok. Add 1-teaspoon cumin seeds. When the seeds crackle and float add sliced ginger and cook for thirty seconds. Add sliced onions and sauté until wilted and yellow. Add one chopped chili pepper and cook for 10 seconds. Add boiled chhole. Sprinkle pomegranate seeds and 1/3 of the mixed dry spices evenly on chhole. Mix and cook for 10 minutes. Add the reserved liquid, add water, if needed to make at least one cup of liquid. Pour liquid along the inside wall of the pot and not over the chhole mix. This is important to prevent washing spices down to the bottom of the pot. Cover and cook for 10 minutes. Stir and check for consistency. *Chhole should be loose in thick gravy and not floating in water, nor should they be dry.* Remove to a serving dish and pour tamarind water over the chhole, mix well. Sprinkle 1/3 of dry spice mix over the surface of chhole.

Mix 1 ½ teaspoons salt to the dry spice mix and use it to evenly coat the fried potato wedges. Arrange fried potatoes on the periphery and garnish the preparation with cilantro, tomato and lemon wedges, thin long slices of hot green pepper and red onion soaked in lemon juice. Serve with puris, chapatis or bhaturas. Serves 12-16.

Bhel (*Bhel Puri*)

4 cups puffed rice (murmura)
¼ cup finely chopped boiled potatoes
1-2 tablespoons finely chopped onions
3 tablespoons besan sev
Salt, to taste

Cayenne pepper to taste (optional)
4 tablespoons cilantro chutney (dhania chutney)
6 tablespoons date chutney (mithi chutney)
½ to 1 teaspoon garlic chutney
¼ teaspoon fresh lime juice
2 tablespoons cilantro, finely chopped
Besan sev or any other sev

In a mixing bowl add puffed rice, potatoes, onions and sev. Mix gently. Add salt, cayenne pepper, chutneys and few drops of lime juice. Mix well. Serve in a bowl and garnish with sev and chopped cilantro.

Refer recipes for cilantro and date chutneys in Chutney section. Besan Sev is available at any Indian grocery store. The following ingredients can be adjusted as per your taste: potatoes, onions, chutneys, salt and lime juice.

Dahi Vadas *(Lentil Dumplings in Yogurt)*

Dahi

1 cup plain whole -milk yogurt
1 cup buttermilk
1 teaspoon sugar
¾ teaspoon salt
¼ teaspoon pepper
½ teaspoon cumin powder

Vadas

1 cup urad dal, soaked
¾ cup water
1 teaspoon salt
Oil for deep frying

Grind soaked dal in a food processor using a small amount of water. Add salt and mix well with a whisk. Heat oil to 325°F. Take 1 tablespoon of dough and drop as a ball in hot oil and fry until golden brown on all sides. Repeat with rest of the dough. Remove and add to a bowl of warm water. Mix dahi ingredients together. Squeeze water from vadas and drain. Add to the yogurt mixture. Serve garnished with paprika and with sweet and sour chutney. Makes 25 to 30 vadas.

Moong Dal Dahi Vadas

Use 32- ounce container of yogurt with 1 tablespoon sugar and 1 teaspoon salt for the yogurt sauce dahi. Omit pepper and cumin powder. Make vadas with 1 cup of hulled mung lentils (yellow moong dal) and follow the above procedure.

Fruit Chaat *(Spicy Fruit and Vegetable Salad)*

In India, fruit chaat is often served by roadside vendors and may consist of roasted sweet potatoes or mixed fruit like apples, bananas, oranges, and guavas along with boiled potatoes. This is usually sprinkled with a mixture of spices and lemon juice. Chaat masala gets its distinctive taste from black salt, roasted cumin, cayenne and mango powder. Salads are always very popular and the addition of garbanzo beans gives extra protein in the vegetarian diet.

1 green apple
1 red apple
1 cucumber
2 Roma tomatoes
1 large peach
1 (15-ounce) can garbanzo beans
½ cup drained crushed pineapple
2 tablespoons fresh lemon juice
2 teaspoons chaat masala
1 teaspoon salt
¼ teaspoon black pepper

Dice all fruits and vegetables. Rinse and drain the garbanzo beans. Mix all the ingredients and serve fresh or refrigerate to use as an appetizer or salad. Serves 8.

Khasta Kachauri

1 cup urad dal
1 tablespoon fennel seeds, coarsely ground
1 teaspoon coriander powder
½ teaspoons garam masala
1/3 teaspoon salt
1/3 teaspoon mango powder
¼ teaspoon hot red pepper
Pinch asafetida
2 tablespoons oil
3 cups all purpose flour
1 teaspoon salt
½ cup vegetable oil
1 cup luke-warm water
Oil for frying

Toast urad dal in a flat heavy bottom skillet on medium heat for about 10 minutes until golden -brown. Cool and coarsely grind in a coffee grinder. Add spices and mix well. Add oil and mix until evenly moistened. Sift flour and salt in a bowl. Add vegetable oil and mix with hand until oil is evenly incorporated into the flour. Make a well in the center of the flour and add water, a little at a time while mixing. Knead gently for 3 minutes, oil hands to ease kneading. Divide dough into 4 portions and cover with a damp cloth. Divide one portion into 10 and roll into balls. Moisten palm of the left hand and fingers of the right hand with oil. Place dough ball in the left hand and flatten into a 2-inch disk by pressing with fingers and heel of the right hand. Place one teaspoon filling in the center of the disk, fold from all sides into the middle and pinch together to seal and secure the filling. Roll gently into 2½ inch circle with a rolling pin or by hand. Deep fry. Heat oil 3 inches deep in a wok to 350 °F. Place kachauries, as many as will fit in a single layer in hot oil, seam side down. Turn over once, lower the heat to 300°F and finish frying until golden brown for about 10 minutes on one side and about 8-9 minutes on the other side. Drain on paper towels. Serve hot or cold with tea or as a part of a chaat table with sweet tamarind chutney, mint chutney and yogurt sauce. Sprinkle with toasted and ground cumin seeds, red and black pepper, salt and chopped cilantro. Makes 40.

Pani Puri *(Gol Guppa or Puchka)*

Potato masala

4 large potatoes boiled, peeled and mashed coarsely
¼ cup kala chana (black gram)
¼ cup chopped cilantro
3-4 teaspoons salt
1 teaspoon cayenne pepper

For Pani

1 cup dry packed tamarind or 2-3 cups canned unsweetened pulp
2 cups packed fresh mint leaves
1½ cups packed cilantro, discard tough stems
3 -inch piece ginger, peeled
7-8 hot serrano peppers
2 teaspoons salt
2 teaspoons black salt
5 teaspoons cumin seeds, roasted and ground
¼ teaspoon black pepper
12-14 cups water, divided

Wash and soak chana overnight in plenty of water. Boil for 15 minutes until soft or pressure cook for one whistle. Mix Potato Masala ingredients in a bowl.

Wash and soak tamarind overnight in 2 cups water, or use boiling water and soak for 2-3 hours. Mash tamarind and put through a coarse strainer/sieve catching the pulp in a bowl. Add 1 cup water to the tamarind in the strainer, mash and strain again until only fibers and seeds remain. Or use the canned pulp. Blend mint, cilantro, ginger and pepper with just enough pulp to make a fine paste. Mix paste, pulp and all spices in a large jar/bowl. Add rest of the water and refrigerate overnight for flavors to blend. For thicker and stronger flavor, reduce the amount of water used. Taste for heat and salt. Add more peppers if not hot enough. Use cayenne pepper if serrano peppers are too mild.

To assemble Pani Puri

Serve 7-8 puris, ¼ cup of potato masala and 1 cup of water.

Tap a hole with a spoon or index finger on the thinner side of the puffed puri, leaving broken pieces in the puri. Place a teaspoon of potato masala in the puri. Stir the water, dunk the puri filling it to the top and pop into the mouth! If not eaten right away, it will get soggy and start disintegrating in a gooey mess.

Use glass or non-reactive bowls. No copper or aluminum bowls, as tamarind will react with these metals. Canned pulp is usually available at Asian stores. Puris are available at most Indian grocers.

For a quick treat, buy puris, tamarind chutney and pani concentrate in Indian stores. A potato can be chopped and cooked in the microwave and used as a filling. Follow directions on chutney bottles.

Anecdote

Growing up in Patna, we were not allowed to eat at roadside vendors for fear of getting sick. When I went to college in Calcutta, I kept hearing about our great canteen and the best pani puris that could be found there; how the local moms would come in their chauffeur driven cars, half an hour early, simply so that they could eat pani puris before picking up their wards. I finally gave in to temptation and with a few friends went to eat pani puris.

The vendor had everything arranged neatly in an assembly line fashion. The puris were to his extreme left, in a huge covered basket, next to the bowl with the potato masala and then the huge earthenware jar of pani. The vendor assembled the pani puris with lightning speed, grabbing a puri in his left hand, popping the top with his thumb, stuffing the masala with his right hand, dunking the whole puri in the pani jar and ultimately lifting out the puri brimming with the spicy, mouth-watering pani. He could feed ten people standing in a semi-circle, with people joining in or stopping at random, within five minutes and charge each one for the exact number of puris consumed.

The four of us stood around holding on to the bowl (This is a large disposable bowl made with bio-degradable leaf, folded into a cone and secured with a tiny wooden pick), while the vendor started assembling the puris. The first puri hit my mouth with fiery abandon, burning my throat and bringing tears to my eyes. Before I could recover, he had sent another puri flying in to my bowl and another and yet another, while I valiantly tried to keep pace by stuffing them into my mouth. I finally motioned a weak 'no more' to the vendor. With my throat on fire, I ran across to the ice cream stall and bought the biggest ice cream. I swore I would eat no more pani puris while my friends shouted with laughter. My resolve lasted just about 24 hours.

Pav Bhaji

Pav Bhaji ('Pav'-Bread and 'Bhaji'-Vegetables) doesn't sound too exciting when put this way but hundreds of people relish it off the hawkers on the pavements in India. Enjoy it as a snack or a complete meal. Top with a dollop of butter and enjoy its with a warm buttered bread roll.

½ pound potatoes
1 can (14-15 oz) green beans
8 oz tomato sauce or 2 cans (8 oz) diced tomatoes
8 tablespoons oil
½ cups onion, finely diced
1 teaspoon garlic, minced
¼ teaspoon cloves, powdered
2 teaspoons coriander powder
½ teaspoon black pepper, freshly ground
½ to ¾ tsp to cinnamon powder
3 tablespoons Pav Bhaji Masala
1 teaspoon cayenne pepper
1 teaspoon salt, or to taste
4 soft bread rolls
2 tablespoons butter

Boil and peel the potatoes. Mash potatoes, beans and tomatoes coarsely. Heat oil in a large saucepan. Sauté the onions for about 3 minites or until the onion is translucent. Add cloves, coriander powder, black pepper, cinnamon, pavbhaji masala, cayenne pepper and salt and sauté for 3 minutes. Now add vegetables and 1 cup water and simmer the curry on low heat for 8 minutes. Mix well and take it off the heat. Slice bread rolls into halves and toast them. Apply butter and serve the curry with bread rolls either placing the curry between the two slices or just beside the rolls. Top with lemon, butter and finely diced onions.

Pav Bhaji Masala is available in Indian grocery stores. Badshah brand is preferred.

Quick Samosas

Samosa are a favorite appetizer and snack. Use of store bought tortillas instead of making and rolling pastry for the covering, offers a quick and easy method for samosas.

4-5 medium sized potatoes, (about 1 pound) boiled, peeled and mashed
1 to 1½ teaspoons salt or to taste
2 teaspoons mango powder
½ teaspoon ground fennel seeds
2 serrano peppers, seeded and chopped (optional)
1 teaspoon garam masala
¼ cup frozen peas, boiled and drained
3 tablespoons all-purpose flour
3 tablespoons water
4-5 Azteca brand flour tortillas

Add salt, mango powder, fennel, serrano peppers and garam masala to the potatoes and mix well. Add peas and mix gently. Make a paste with all-purpose flour and water. Cut flour tortillas into two. Make a cone or a triangle, with slightly overlapping edges and use the flour paste to seal the cut side in the center. Fill with 2 tablespoons of filling. Seal the open edge of the cone or triangle with the paste. Keep aside and cover with damp cloth to prevent them from drying out. Repeat with remaining tortillas.

Heat oil to 320°F on medium heat. Fry samosas until the covering is golden. Drain on paper towels. Serve hot with cilantro chutney.

Azteca brand flour tortillas are preferred as they are thinner than other tortillas. Warm the tortilla for a few seconds in the microwave to make it softer and pliable.

Tomato-Kaju Idli

1 cup sooji (semolina)
1 ½ tablespoons oil
1 cup plain yogurt
½ cup water
3/4 teaspoon salt
½ teaspoon baking soda
1 small tomato
4-5 cashew nuts, halved
8-10 kari leaves (kadi patta or sweet neem leaves)

Heat oil in a microwave safe dish for 1 minute at full power. Add sooji, mix well and microwave for 2 minutes. Mix well and add salt, mix again and allow to cool. Add water and yogurt and mix to a smooth batter. Add baking soda; mix well and let stand for 10 minutes in a warm place. Grease 6 microwavable idli moulds or custard cups. Place a piece of tomato; a cashew crescent and one kari leaf at the bottom of the mold. Place 3-4 tablespoons of idli batter into each mold and microwave uncovered for 3½ minutes. Let stand for 5 minutes before serving. Empty mold, bottom up, on to a serving dish. The tomato, cashew and kari leaf make great eye appeaser. Serve with ghee or sambar and/or coconut chutney or, ghee and shakkar (powdered sugar). Makes 6.

Kari leaves, Curry leaves, Sweet Neem, Kadi Patta, Kari Patta, Meetha Neem. These green leaves are available fresh as well as dried. The fresh leaves are often sold on the stem. They may be frozen for a couple of months. Will last in the refrigerator for a couple of weeks in a ziplock bag. Is used heavily in cuisine of south and western India. The leaves are used whole for baghar and often along with stems in dals.

Vadas

These legume fritters are a very popular snack in Southern India as well as south Louisiana.

2 cups split peas or chana dal
4 long hot green chili peppers
1 inch piece fresh ginger, peeled and coarsely chopped
1 cup red onion, coarsely chopped
30 fresh kari leaves (kadi patta)
2 teaspoons salt or to taste
6 cups vegetable oil to deep fry

Clean, wash and soak the dal in 6 cups of warm water for 2 hours or overnight in tap water. Drain and save 3 tablespoons and grind the remaining dal coarsely in a food processor with ginger. Remove to a large mixing bowl. Add green chillies, onion, and kari leaves along with 3 tablespoons of chana dal and process to a coarse mixture. Mix well with the rest of the ground dal. Add 2 teaspoons of salt just prior to making the vadas. Mix well. Heat oil in deep fryer or electric wok (400 °F) to a height of 3 inches. Make 1 ½- inch balls with about 1 tablespoon of dough, binding this together in the palm of your right hand. Then put the ball in the palm of your left hand and with the fingers of the right hand flatten it to a thick disc so that the edges are thinner and the center is thicker. Slip it into the hot oil and deep fry several at a time turning them 3 or 4 times so that they brown evenly. Remove when they are golden brown and drain on paper towels. Keep lightly covered with foil when cooled. Serve hot or at room temperature, with cilantro chutney or ketchup. Makes 40 pieces.

Can be frozen and reheated in an oven at 350° F temperature for 20 minutes.

Soups and Salads

Carrot Soup

1 pound baby carrots
1 ½ cups peeled and diced potatoes
1 ½ teaspoon salt
4 cups water
2 teaspoons oil
1 tablespoon finely chopped onion
1 clove garlic, crushed and chopped
1 cup chicken broth or vegetable stock
½ cup Half and Half cream, divided
½ teaspoon Tabasco sauce
Dash cayenne pepper
1 teaspoon black pepper
1 tablespoon butter
1 tablespoon basil or cilantro, divided
½ teaspoon paprika

In a 3-quart microwave-safe saucepan, place carrots, potatoes, salt and water. Cover and microwave on full power for 20-25 minutes until carrots are soft. *(Carrots take longer to cook)*. Sauté onions and garlic until onions are translucent. *(Browned onions will discolor the soup)*. Add broth/ vegetable stock. Boil for 1 minute. Add broth/stock to the cooked vegetables. Blend vegetable mixture in a blender until smooth. Add half and half cream. Cook for 2 more minutes while stirring. *(Mixture may spatter)* Add Tabasco sauce, cayenne pepper, 1/4 teaspoon black pepper and 1 teaspoon chopped cilantro. Add butter and mix well. Pour in a soup bowl. Add 1tablespoon hot half and half cream in the center and swirl with a knife. To garnish, sprinkle freshly ground black pepper, paprika and a sprig of cilantro/basil. Tastes great with green salad and garlic bread or soda crackers. Serve hot! Serves 8.

Suggestions
May add a few drops of red food color after removing from the heat.

Gujarati Kadhi *(Yogurt Soup)*

2 cups sour yogurt
2 tablespoons chickpea flour (besan)
4 cups water
1 teaspoon minced ginger
½ teaspoon minced garlic
2 tablespoons sugar
¾ teaspoon salt, to taste
Baghar
1 tablespoon oil
1- inch cinnamon stick
5 cloves
½ teaspoon mustard seeds
½ teaspoon fenugreek seeds (methi)
½ teaspoon cumin seeds
8-10 kari leaves with stalks
1 serrano pepper, finely chopped (optional)
Pinch of asafetida (hing)
2 teaspoons cilantro, finely chopped

Whip yogurt and add enough water to obtain a pouring consistency. Add chickpea flour to ½ cup of diluted yogurt; mix well until there are no lumps. Add this mixture to the rest of the diluted yogurt. A hand blender can be used to mix. To the yogurt mixture, add ginger, garlic, sugar and salt to taste. Heat oil in a saucepan over moderate heat. Add cinnamon, cloves, mustard seeds, fenugreek seeds, cumin seeds and the kari leaves. Add Serrano peppers and lastly asafetida. Finally, add yogurt mixture and stir constantly until it boils, then cook on low heat for 10 to 15 minutes. Add chopped cilantro prior to removing it from heat. Serve with rice or as a soup. Serves 4 to 5.

To enhance the taste of the kadhi, extend the boiling time. Kadhi has a tendency to boil over, so keep a close eye, and cook on low heat. Stir often so the chickpea flour will not stick to the bottom. Yogurt will become sour if left on a counter top for several hours. Homemade yogurt tends to become sour much faster than the one bought from the store.

Red Bell Pepper Soup

3 large red bell peppers
2 tomatoes
1 teaspoon salt
½ cup water
1 clove garlic
½ cup milk

Steam the bell peppers, tomatoes and garlic with salt and water. Puree in a blender and strain. Add milk and cook for a few minutes. Garnish with fresh basil, rosemary, grated Parmesan cheese and fresh ground black pepper to taste.

Yogurt Soup with Pakoras

½ cup chickpea flour (besan)
1 cup yogurt
1 quart buttermilk
2 teaspoon coriander powder
2 teaspoon turmeric
1 teaspoon cayenne pepper
1 tablespoon mango powder (amchur)
1½ quarts water
2 teaspoons salt
2-3 tablespoons oil
1 teaspoon cumin seeds
1 cup finely chopped onion
1 tablespoon ginger, freshly grated
2 Serrano peppers, seeded and finely chopped
4 cloves garlic, chopped
1 teaspoon fenugreek leaves (kasuri methi) (optional)
Pinch of asafetida (hing) (optional)

Spice infused oil

1 tablespoon butter
1 teaspoon oil
1 tablespoon garam masala
1 teaspoon paprika
2 tablespoon fresh cilantro, chopped

Dumplings

1 cup chickpea flour (besan)
1 onion, chopped
1 teaspoon garam masala
1 hot green chili pepper, chopped
1 teaspoon salt
1 tablespoon oil
Oil for frying

Yogurt Soup

Mix besan with yogurt, buttermilk and spices. Stir well to remove lumps. Heat oil in a 6 quart pan; add cumin, roast for 30 seconds. Add asafetida and fenugreek leaves, if using. Immediately add onion, ginger, pepper, and garlic. Stir-fry for 3-4 minutes on medium heat. Add yogurt mixture to the pan and stir thoroughly. Add all the water to the mix and bring to a boil. Lower heat and cook for 20 minutes, stirring frequently. Adjust salt and pepper. Pour in a serving bowl. Add dumplings. In a sauté pan heat oil and butter, add garam masala and paprika. Swirl and pour over the soup along with chopped cilantro. Serve with plain rice.

Dumplings

Mix all ingredients and make a thick pancake like batter. Heat oil and drop dumplings by spoonful into hot oil. Fry to golden brown. Drain on paper towels. Addition of dumplings is optional, but desired. Serves 8-10.

Spinach Virshe (Spinach Soup)

This is a light spinach soup with an unusual flavor. It is given to nursing mothers in Karwar, South India to stimulate their appetite, as well as to provide an extra source of iron.

1 (10 ounce) package frozen spinach
½ teaspoon carom seeds (ajwain)
½ teaspoon freshly ground black pepper
4 cups water
½ serrano chili pepper, seeded
2 teaspoons salt
1 to 2 tablespoon lemon juice
2 large cloves garlic, sliced
1 tablespoon ghee or butter

Cook spinach in a microwave according to package directions. Roast ajwain and pepper in a small skillet on medium heat for 1-2 minutes. Powder the spices. Puree the spinach and serrano chili in a food processor or a blender, using 2 cups of water. Pour the pureed spinach in a two quart saucepan. Add 2 more cups of water. Add ground spices, salt and lemon juice. Bring to boil and simmer for 2 minutes. Heat butter or clarified butter in a small skillet on medium heat. Add sliced garlic and cook until garlic is crisp and caramelized. Pour into the soup. Stir and check soup for seasoning. Serve hot.

Flavor is best the day it is made. Adding caramalized garlic just before serving, will keep it crisp. Thyme may be substituted for ajwain.

Tomato Saar (South Indian Tomato Soup)

1 pound fresh tomatoes (2 large)) or 1 (14 ounce) can diced tomatoes
3 cups water
1 serrano chili pepper
1 ½ teaspoons salt
2 teaspoons brown sugar
For Tadka
1 teaspoon oil or ghee
½ teaspoon mustard seeds
Pinch of asafetida (hing)
2 dried red chilies
4-5 fresh kari leaves

In a 2-quart saucepan, cook tomatoes and green chili in boiling water for 10 to 15 minutes. Cool, blend and strain to remove seeds and skin. Add salt and brown sugar.

For Tadka

Heat oil or ghee in a small skillet over medium heat. Add mustard seeds, asafetida, chilies and kari leaves. Remove from heat when mustard seeds begin to pop. Add to hot soup. Serve in a cup as a starter. Serves 4.

Pumpkin Soup

2 tablespoons butter
1 medium onion, chopped
2 cloves garlic, peeled and mashed
½ inch piece of ginger, peeled and grated
1 small potato, boiled and peeled
2 cups pumpkin, cubed and cooked (or 1 pound canned pumpkin)
2 cups water (or chicken stock, optional)
1 teaspoon salt
¼ to ½ teaspoon cinnamon
1 tablespoon toasted pumpkin seeds
1 tablespoon crabmeat (optional)
½ teaspoon black pepper
¼ cup cream (optional)

Heat a saucepan on medium. Add butter and onions. Sauté until onions are soft. Add garlic, ginger, pumpkin and potato. Mix well and add water or chicken stock, salt and cinnamon. Bring to boil and simmer for 15 minutes. Mash or puree in a blender.

Stir in the cream and black pepper and top with pumpkin seeds or crabmeat. Serves 6-8.

Do not boil once cream is added. Cooking after black pepper is added makes the soup bitter.

Rasam *(Tomato Lentil Soup)*

Rasam is a flavored, light dal soup. Different kinds are made daily in South India.

1 teaspoon oil
1 teaspoon mustard seeds
5 cups water
¾ cup split yellow peas
¼ tsp turmeric
1/8 teaspoon asafetida
4 teaspoon sambhar powder
1 medium tomato chopped or 8 oz canned diced tomato
1 teaspoon tamarind paste
2 teaspoon dark brown sugar
1 and ½ teaspoon salt
½ cup chopped fresh cilantro

Heat a 3-quart saucepan on high, add oil and mustard seeds. Cover the pan until mustard seeds have popped (about 30 seconds). Add water and bring to a boil. Wash the peas, drain and add to the boiling water. Cover, reduce heat to medium and cook until peas are soft (about 45 minutes). Add turmeric, asafetida, sambhar powder and tomatoes.

Cook for 10 minutes. Add tamarind paste. Cooks for another 10 minutes. Add brown sugar, salt and stir to dissolve. Stir in fresh cilantro, just before serving. Serve hot in mugs as an appetizer or as soup. Serves 8.

Sambhar powder can be purchased from an Indian grocer. M.T.R. brand is preferred.

Tomato Soup

4 large tomatoes or 12 ounces diced canned tomatoes
5 cups water
1 small onion, chopped medium
2 cloves garlic
1 teaspoon salt
1 small potato, peeled and cubed
2 tablespoon butter
1 teaspoon sugar
Black pepper to taste
½ teaspoon garam masala
2 tablespoons cilantro, chopped
Crême Fraîche

Boil water in a pan. Score the tomatoes in a cross and drop them in boiling water for 30 seconds. Remove tomatoes and plunge them in cold water, thereby loosening their skin. Remove the skin and chop the tomatoes. Add water along with potato, onion, garlic and salt. Cook for 20 minutes on low heat. Puree the soup in a blender in batches and strain to remove any seeds. Melt butter in a saucepan. Add to that black pepper, salt and pureed soup. Add cilantro and garam masala and warm the soup.

Adjust salt and pepper. Serve warm, topped with a dollop of Crême Fraiche and cilantro. Serves 4.

To make Crême Fraîche: Mix 8 ounces sour cream with 1 cup of heavy cream and let sit on the kitchen counter for 12 to 24 hours until thickened. Refrigerate and use within 1 week.

Cucumber Salad

1 large cucumber, peeled & diced
½ to 1 serrano pepper, finely chopped
3 tablespoons roasted peanuts or soy nuts, crushed
2 tablespoons coconut, grated
Salt, to taste
½ teaspoon sugar or to taste

Finely grate or dice the cucumber and remove excess water. Add Serrano pepper, nuts, coconut and mix well. Add salt and sugar just prior to serving and mix well.

Salt and sugar bring out water from the cucumber. Addition of these just prior to serving prevents the salad from becoming soggy.

Koshimbir (Mixed Vegetable Salad)

1 small cabbage
4 medium carrots, peeled
2 medium tomatoes
¼ cup yellow hulled mung dal (dhuli moong dal)
3 tablespoons oil
½ teaspoon mustard seeds
¼ teaspoon asafetida
1 small hot green chili, chopped (optional)
¼ teaspoon cayenne pepper
1 tablespoon lemon juice
¼ teaspoon sugar

Rinse and soak moong dal two hours before preparing the salad. To properly soak moong dal, keep water level about two inches above dal. Grate cabbage and carrots. Chop tomatoes very finely. Mix vegetables in a large bowl. Heat oil in a small skillet on medium heat. Add mustard seeds. When they begin to pop, add asafetida, turmeric powder and chopped green chilies and sauté for about 1 minute. This process is called "tadka" or "phodni". Remove from heat. Drain water from dal. Mix cabbage, carrots, tomato, dal, salt, sugar, cayenne pepper, tadka and lemon juice.

Garnish with chopped cilantro. Serves 6 people, ½ cup each. This is a very delicious, tasty and nutritious salad.

Sonth Salad (Ginger Salad)

1 Granny Smith apple
1 cup red grapes
1 navel orange
½ cup water chestnuts
2 teaspoons salad vinegar
1 tablespoon fresh lime juice
1 teaspoon ginger powder (sonth)
2 tablespoons coconut powder, divided
1 teaspoon sea salt (black salt may be used)
Dash cayenne pepper
1 teaspoon black pepper

Cut apples into thin wedges, cut grapes in half, peel orange and separate into segments.

Cut water chestnuts in half. Mix first seven ingredients and 1 tablespoon coconut powder. Place in a serving bowl and refrigerate until ready to serve. Immediately before serving, sprinkle sea salt, cayenne pepper and freshly ground black pepper. Garnish with remaining coconut powder. Serves 4. May be used as a midmorning snack, at teatime or with meals. Excellent with ginger chicken.

Tomato Cucumber Bean Sprout Salad

1 large firm tomato
1 cucumber
½ cup bean sprouts
½ head of lettuce, finely cut
1 to 2 serrano peppers
1 tablespoon lime or lemon juice
1 tablespoon olive oil
½ teaspoon sugar
Salt and pepper to taste
2 tablespoons chopped cilantro, optional

Wash, de-seed, and cut tomato into ½ -inch cubes. Peel, de-seed cucumber and cut into same size as tomato pieces. De-seed and chop peppers very fine & crush with salt. Mix limejuice, sugar and olive oil. In a medium bowl mix all the ingredients and toss well. Chopped cilantro may be added for extra flavor.

Tea Time

Tea time

Tea or 'chai' as it is commonly called, is indigenous to the Indian sub continent with plenty of tea plantations on the east coast of India. Tea-time, however, is a legacy of the British Raj. The British established East Indian Trading Company to harvest and ship teas and spices from India. Assam and Darjeeling produce some of the finest teas in the world. The tea leaves are hand picked and blended to suit individual tastes. The British left India half a century ago, but have left behind a population of habitual tea drinkers. There are as many ways as people to make tea and every family has a tea ritual. Some folks like to mix water, tea and milk together and bring it to a boil. The concoction is then strained, sweetened & served. Others prefer to steep tea leaves in boiling water, strain and serve with milk or lemon, sweet or un-sweet. Some folks flavor their tea with chai masala which may or may not contain saffron, ginger or cardamom.

Tea is served at all times of the day, in-between meals or whenever guests drop by. Morning and afternoon tea have become a tradition in most homes. Afternoon tea is usually served after siesta, includes various savory and sweet snacks and is used to hold one over until supper, which is often served after 8 PM.

Some of the snacks served at teatime are: Aloo dal vada, Cake, Cheese sticks, Chumchum, Gulab jamun, Muruku, Pakoras, Poha, Potato muffins, Samosas, Chewda, Tea biscuits and Upma. The recipes are included in the book.

Almond Pecan Cookies

2 cups all-purpose flour
1 cup unsalted butter
2/3 cup sugar
1/3 cup ground almonds
1/3 cup ground pecans

Preheat oven to 350°F. Mix all ingredients. Make 1-inch balls and place on a cookie sheet and bake at 350°F for 25 minutes. Cool completely. Store in an airtight container.

Aloo Bhajia (Sliced Potato Fritters)

The monsoon season in India is called 'Varsha Ritu'. Dark clouds, cooler weather after the scorching summer, a light drizzle and the fresh smell of damp earth all evoke a special feeling. You often hear these words…perfect weather for bhajias or pakoras!

2 large russet potatoes, washed and sliced very thin
1½ cups chickpea flour (besan)
½ cup rice flour
2 teaspoons salt
1 teaspoon cayenne pepper
Pinch of baking soda
5-6 drops lemon juice
¾ cup water
Oil for frying

Use russet potatoes and do not peel. Slice very thin using mandolin or food processor.

Soak in water. Rinse and dry using paper towels. Make a batter by mixing chickpea flour, rice flour, salt, cayenne, baking soda and lemon juice. Add water and mix well to make a smooth batter. Dip potatoes in the batter one at a time and let excess batter drip off and slip it into the hot oil. Deep fry potato slices on medium heat, several pieces at a time. The batter coating will puff slightly. Turn the slices to brown both sides. The same batter recipe can be used for other vegetables, such as cauliflower florets, sliced eggplant, squash and zucchini. Cauliflower florets can be partially cooked in the microwave to ensure they are well cooked in the center. Serve hot, with cilantro or mint chutney.

Aloo Bonda *(Batata Vada)*

1 pound potatoes, boiled, peeled and mashed
1 hot green chili pepper, chopped
1 ½ teaspoons salt
1 teaspoon garam masala
1 tablespoon mango powder (amchur)
1 teaspoon coriander/cumin powder mixture
1 tablespoon sugar
1 small onion, finely chopped and sautéed in oil till translucent (optional)
2 cloves garlic, chopped and sautéed, (optional)

For the Batter

2 cups chickpea flour (besan)
2 teaspoons salt
Pinch of baking soda
5-6 drops lemon juice
1 ½ cups water
Oil for deep-frying

In a medium bowl, mash potatoes. Add chopped green chilies, salt, garam masala, mango powder, coriander and cumin powder and sugar and mix well. Add onion and garlic, if using. Make 20 one-inch balls. Cover and set aside. In another medium bowl, mix chickpea flour with salt, baking soda, lemon juice and water until all lumps have disappeared. Dip balls in batter and deep fry on medium-high heat until the coating is golden brown (about 2 minutes). Drain on a paper towel. Serve hot, with cilantro or date chutney.

Chakli *(Rice Crunchies)*

Savory snacks are very popular in India and are served with an afternoon cup of tea. This dish, also called Muruku is traditionally made with a single star disc. It is much easier to use a 3-hole spaghetti type disc. This particular recipe comes from the southern part of India.

1 cup rice flour
1/8 cup urad dal flour
3 tablespoons melted butter or margarine
1 teaspoon cumin seeds
1 teaspoon sesame seeds
Salt to taste (slightly more than 1 teaspoon)
1/4 cup water
Oil for frying
Cookie press

Mix all ingredients except oil and knead into a soft dough. Heat oil in a small wok or 10 inch deep skillet to about 300°F. Test temperature of oil by dropping a small piece of dough. It should sizzle up to the surface within a couple of seconds, but not turn brown immediately. Use cookie press and select a disc with 3 holes. Squeeze the dough directly into hot oil, making the shape of a small pretzel. Fry 2 or 3 pretzels at a time on medium heat, turning once, until golden brown on both sides. Drain on paper towels. The heat may have to be adjusted occasionally to maintain proper temperature of the oil. Serve as an appetizer or with afternoon tea.

Store in an airtight container at room temperature for several days. Can also be frozen.

Cheese Fingers

¾ cup all-purpose flour
½ cup sharp cheddar cheese, grated
4 tablespoons butter, melted
1 teaspoon jalapeno pepper, finely chopped
¼ teaspoon cayenne pepper
Pinch of ajwain
1 egg yolk, beaten
1 teaspoon parsley flakes

Combine first six ingredients in a bowl; mix gently so that the ingredients form a ball. Do not knead. Roll out to about ¼ inch thick rectangle. Brush egg yolk on the surface. Sprinkle with parsley flakes. Cut into 4 inch by ½ inch pieces. Place on an ungreased cookie sheet, and bake at 400 degrees for 10 to 12 minutes or until golden brown. Makes 2 dozen.

Corn Flakes Chewra

4 tablespoons oil
1 teaspoon mustard seeds
1 teaspoon cumin seeds
1/8 teaspoon asafetida
4 teaspoons sesame seeds
6 teaspoons fennel seeds
1 cup nuts (peanuts, cashew nuts, etc.)
2 cups raisins
1 (20 ounce) large packet corn flakes
2 teaspoons black salt
1 teaspoon turmeric
2 teaspoons citric acid crystals
4 teaspoons sugar

Heat oil, mustard seeds and cumin seeds in a large pan and them let crackle. Add asafetida sizzle for a few seconds. Add sesame seeds, fennel seeds and nuts & toast to brown. Add raisins and cornflakes. Add black salt, salt, turmeric, citric acid and sugar. Cook on low heat for 10 min. Cool and store in a tight jar in a dry place. Serve with tea or as a snack anytime.

Coconut Biscuits *(Coconut Cookies)*

Cookies or biscuits as they are called in India always accompany a cup of tea. Although a variety of cookies are now available in the neighborhood store, homemade ones are always special.

1 can (14-ounce) sweetened condensed milk
½ cup semolina (sooji)
1 bag Mounds coconut or fresh grated coconut
1 cup finely chopped pecans
¼ cup golden raisins
1 stick (4 ounces) butter
Vegetable shortening spray

Mix all the ingredients together. Make balls, about 1-inch in diameter. Place on a cookie sheet, lined with parchment paper sprayed with vegetable shortening. Bake at 350°F for about 20 minutes or until golden brown. Remove from oven and cool on a rack.

Makes 30 biscuits.

Coconut Burfi

Nostalgia from college days. The smell of toasted coconut made teatime a coveted delight.

3 cups sugar
3 cups water
2 cans (12 ounces each) evaporated milk
½ cup raw cashew nuts, coarsely chopped
1½ cup magaz (melon seeds) divided, save 1 tablespoon for garnish
3 cups shredded coconut, divided, save 1 tablespoon for garnish
2 teaspoons cardamom seeds
2 tablespoons unsalted butter
1 teaspoon vanilla extract

Place sugar in a 6-quart stainless steel pot. Pour evaporated milk and water in it. **Don't stir.** Bring the mixture to a rolling boil on high heat. Then lower the heat and continue boiling until temperature reaches 235°F (soft ball consistency). Add cashew nuts and magaz, stir for 2 to 3 seconds and add coconut and cardamom seeds. Immediately remove from heat, add butter and vanilla, mix thoroughly and quickly pour into a buttered tray. Flatten to about ½ inch thick rectangle. Toast magaz and coconut and garnish. Cut into 1½- inch square pieces while still warm. Cool completely in a basket or a rack. Store in an airtight jar. In wintertime, it will last for 1 month at room temperature. Great for teatime, eat one, eat two…!

Dahi Toast *(Yogurt Toast)*

A quick snack or light lunch with a unique flavor.

4-5 tablespoons thick plain yogurt
2 tablespoons sugar
Salt to taste
8 slices bread, any kind
Red or black pepper to taste
3 tablespoons oil
1 tablespoon mustard seeds
Kari leaves (optional)

Mix salt, pepper and sugar into yogurt. Spread liberally on one side of 4 slices of bread. Cover the spread with remaining 4 slices of bread. Cut the sandwiches into four squares each. Heat oil in a non-stick frying pan. Add mustard seeds and cover. When they start popping, add kari leaves and add bread pieces after a few seconds. Shallow fry bread on both sides (about 1 minute each). The bread should be crisp and browned and not soggy. No oil should be left in the pan. Serve immediately. Serves 2-4.

Mathian *(Savory Crackers)*

These savory crackers are made with dough similar to pastry dough. This recipe brings back the taste of Punjab.

2½ cups all-purpose flour
1 teaspoon salt
1 teaspoon thymol/carom seeds (ajwain)
½ cup peanut oil
½ cup lukewarm water
1 tablespoon black peppercorns
Peanut oil for frying

Mix flour, salt and ajwain in a large bowl and work in the oil with hands until evenly dispersed. Gradually add water and make a smooth dough. Divide into 20 balls and roll out or press into 1/8-inch thick discs. Press 4 or 5 evenly spaced peppercorns on each disc. Perforate the discs with a knife or fork to prevent puffing. Pour oil to a depth of 3 inches in a wok. Heat on medium high (350°-355° F). Drop mathian, several at a time, and fry, turning frequently with a perforated spoon until light golden brown. Drain on paper towels. Cool, and store in an airtight container in a cool dry place. Serve as a snack, teatime treat or with drinks.

Ajwain (carom seeds) is the classic spice used in matris but cumin, thyme or crushed rosemary may be substituted. Ajwain is available in Indian grocery stores.

54

Batata Poha (Pressed Rice with Potatoes)

2 cups thick poha,
1 large potato, peeled and sliced into thin
1- inch pieces
1 tablespoon roasted peanuts or use
peanuts with skin and roast in 1
teaspoon oil
8 fresh kari leaves
3-4 tablespoons vegetable oil
¼ teaspoon mustard seeds
½ teaspoon cumin seeds
Pinch of asafetida (hing)
Pinch of turmeric
Lemon juice
1 ¼ cups onion(1 large), finely chopped
1 serrano pepper, chopped
½ teaspoon sugar
4 tablespoons cilantro leaves with tender
stems, chopped
2 tablespoons coconut, fresh or frozen,
thawed and finely grated

Pick over the poha, rinse in a colander and drain well. Add ¾ teaspoon salt, pinch of turmeric, ½ teaspoon sugar and juice of ½ a lemon and mix gently. Peel the potato, cut it into 1x1-inch slices. Wash and drain on a paper towel. Heat ½ tablespoon oil in a sauté pan over moderate heat. Sauté potato slices till cooked for about 5 minutes. Sprinkle ¼ teaspoon salt. Set aside. In a nonstick pan heat 2 tablespoons oil over medium heat. Add mustard, cumin, and asafetida. Stir for 30 seconds, add kari leaves and chopped onions. Cook until onions are transparent or light browned (about 5 minutes). Add a pinch of turmeric powder, peanuts, cooked potato slices and drained poha. Mix well. Cover and cook on low heat for 4-5 minutes. Check seasonings for salt and lemon. Serve garnished with chopped cilantro and grated fresh coconut. Serves 3-4 people.

Poha reheats well in a microwave. May substitute 1 cup cooked peas for the potatoes.
½ cup of uncooked poha makes enough for 1 person.

Sev *(Crispy Chickpea Noodle Snack)*

2 cups chickpea flour (besan), measured before sifting
¼ cup urad dal flour
1 tablespoon vegetable oil
1 teaspoon salt

1 teaspoon cayenne pepper
1 teaspoon carom seeds (ajwain), crushed coarsely
1 cup minus 3 tablespoons water
4 cups vegetable oil to deep fry

Heat 4 cups of oil in a wok or deep skillet, over moderate heat. Sift besan and urad dal flour in a 2-quart bowl. Add 1 tablespoon oil, salt, cayenne, crushed ajwain and water; mix well with a spoon so that there are no lumps. Put the thick dough in a sev mold or cookie press with a noodle disk. Press the sev directly into moderately hot oil, making a circular coil 3 times. Cook for 3minutes until it darkens a little and then turn over, using a slotted spatula. Fry for 2 minutes more. Drain excess oil on the side of the wok. Remove to a paper towel to drain. Repeat process until all dough is used up. Can store in an airtight container for up to 2 weeks at room temperature or can be kept fresh in the freezer for several months. The sev is crushed in to 1-2 inch pieces when served. Serve as a snack at teatime. Makes 6 coils.

Can be mixed with other fried lentils and puffed rice to make chivda. The addition of urad dal flour to makes the sev crisp. Addition of oil to the dough makes the sev tender and crisp.

Shakkar Paare

Little cubes of deep fried pastry coated with sugar is served with tea and on special occasions such as weddings in Punjab. This recipe is an example of using thick sugar syrup in making desserts.

2½ cups all-purpose flour
½ cup peanut oil
½ cup warm milk
Peanut oil to deep fry
For the Syrup
1 ¼ cups sugar
¼ cup water

Mix flour in a bowl and work in the oil by hand until evenly dispersed. Gradually add milk and make smooth dough. Divide dough into four pieces and rollout to ½ inch thick discs. Cut into ¾ inch cubes and fry on medium high heat (350°-355° F), turning frequently, until light brown. Drain shakkar paare on a paper towel and place in a bowl for syrup coating.

Syrup

Mix sugar and water in a saucepan. Place the pan on medium heat and cook, stirring until the sugar liquefies. Continue to cook until mixture is bubbling. Check the drip by holding the stirring spoon up. When the drip forms a single thread, the syrup is ready. Immediately pour the syrup over the shakkar paare and fold to coat. Leave at room temperature and fold every 2 – 3 minutes to evenly coat them. The coating will turn from clear to white as the sugar cools and thickens. Cool and store in an airtight container in a cool dry place.

Tea Biscuits

Ladies in the Punjab mix the ingredients for these cookies or biscuits as they are called in India, in a tall tin box and send them to the neighborhood baker, as it was not common to have an oven at home. A box of mouth-watering cookies would be delivered home in the evening. A plate of these cookies would always be served with evening tea.

4 cups whole wheat or chapati flour
1 pound unsalted butter, softened
2 cups sugar
¼ teaspoons baking soda
2 teaspoons baking powder
¼ cup whole milk
Non-stick cooking spray
1 cookie press

Preheat oven to 350° F. Mix wheat flour, sugar, baking soda and baking powder in a large bowl. Cut in softened butter and mix well. Add milk and mix lightly to make soft dough, similar to roti dough. Spray cookie sheet with cooking spray. Use 1/8-inch thick ribbon die for the cookie press. Press dough through the cookie press and cut in 2 -inch long pieces. Bake at 350°F degrees for 8 to 10 minutes. Cool and store in an airtight container. Serve with tea.

If a cookie press is not available divide the dough into four parts. Make each part into a one inch thick, two inches wide and about four inches long rectangular brick. Keep in the refrigerator to firm the dough. Cut ¼ inch thick cookies and bake as directed.

Makes 4 dozen

Chapati flour is available in Indian grocery stores. Cookies can be frozen.

Upma *(Spicy Cream of Wheat)*

Upma is a South Indian breakfast dish, but it can also be served for lunch or dinner. It is very nutritious and easy to make. The consistency can vary from slightly dry to very moist. Adjust the quantity of water to your preference.

2 tablespoons cooking oil
1 teaspoon mustard seeds
1 teaspoon chana dal
1 teaspoon urad dal
1 tablespoon peanuts
1 tablespoon cashew nuts (optional)
½ teaspoon fresh ginger, chopped
10-12 kari leaves
2 hot green chili peppers, chopped
¼ cup chopped onions
2 cups cream of wheat
2 teaspoons salt on to taste
4 cups water
Fresh coriander leaves for garnish

In a medium sauté pan, heat oil over medium heat. Add mustard seeds, chana dal and urad dal and fry until golden brown. Add peanuts and cashew nuts (optional). Add ginger, kari leaves, chopped onions, green chilies and sauté for 3 to 4 minutes. Add cream of wheat and fry it with other ingredients for 2 to 3 minutes. Add salt and water and mix well. Cook on low heat for 5 to7 minutes. If you like butter flavor, add 1 to 2 tablespoons melted butter on top and garnish with coriander leaves. Serve warm with pickle or chutney. Serves 4 for breakfast or 2 for lunch.

Serve upma with a round big spoon; it looks nice with chutney or omelet on the side.

My personal favorite is with an Indian omelet (two eggs, ¼ cup chopped onions, 1 chopped hot green chili pepper, chopped fresh cilantro, garlic powder and salt to taste.)

Cream of wheat (not instant) or coarse sooji, available at Indian grocery stores may be used. A variation is to use cracked bulghur wheat (dalia). Dry roast it prior to using; may need extra water. You can add chopped vegetables such as, carrots, green peas, tomatoes, potatoes, etc., after you add the onions.

Gobhi Musalam

Vegetarian Dishes

Achari Baingan Bhaji (Spicy Eggplant)

The spices used in this recipe are similar to those used to make achar (pickles) hence the name.

1 eggplant, peeled and diced in
1-inch pieces
1 tablespoon vegetable oil
½ cup diced seasoning mix
(available at grocery stores)
1 tablespoon panch phoran
(five spice mix)
1 teaspoon turmeric
1 teaspoon mango powder (amchur)
1 teaspoon salt
2 tablespoons chopped tomatoes
½ cup water
Chopped cilantro to garnish, optional

Heat a sauté pan on high heat, add oil and seasoning mix. Stir to coat and cook for 2 to 3 minutes. Add all spices and tomato to the mix. Stir and add eggplant. Add water, cover and simmer for 20 minutes or until eggplant is tender. Garnish with chopped cilantro if desired.

Serve as a vegetable with rice, roti or naan, and yogurt. Serves 8.

Look for seasoning mix in the freezer section of your supermarket. It usually contains chopped celery, onion, bell pepper, parsley and garlic.

Beans Upkari *(Green Bean Stirfry)*

Upkari is a way of cooking vegetables from the Saraswats of South India. It is a light stirifried, dish flavored with mustard seeds, urad dal, and hot green peppers. You can substitute finely sliced green cabbage, or summer squash.

1 ½ tablespoon oil
Pinch of asafetida, optional
½ teaspoon mustard seeds
¼ teaspoon urad dal
1 ¼ pound green beans, washed, top and bottom removed and chopped finely
1 teaspoon salt
½ teaspoon sugar
1-2 hot green chili peppers, kept whole

Heat oil in a 2-quart sauté pan or wok over moderate heat. Add mustard seeds and asafetida and let the seeds pop. Add chili pepper and urad dal and stir for 15 seconds until the dal is light brown. Add beans and stir to coat the beans with oil. Sprinkle salt and sugar. Cook uncovered, over low heat stirring occasionally, until the beans are tender and cooked. A few teaspoons of water may be added if the beans are not very tender. However, do not overcook the beans. Sprinkle 2 tablespoons fresh grated coconut prior to serving.

The addition of a pinch of sugar brings out the natural sweetness in the vegetable and balances the flavors.

Broccoli / Spinach Thoran (Broccoli / Spinach Stirfry)

Kerala, in the south-west of India is known for its beautiful backwaters, which are similar to the bayous we find in Louisiana. Traders from the west discovered these shores on their quest for spices eastward. They brought chilis, fenugreek, and cashews, which now feature predominantly in the cuisine of Kerala. Thoran is a stir-fry from this region.

1 ½ tablespoon vegetable oil
½ teaspoon black mustard seed
½ onion, thinly sliced
1 hot green chili pepper, chopped
¼ cup dehydrated coconut
¼ teaspoon turmeric
¼ teaspoon ground cumin
1 (10 ounce) box frozen chopped broccoli or spinach (if using forzen spinach, thaw first)
Salt to taste (about ¾ teaspoon)

In a skillet or wok, heat oil. Add mustard seeds and cook for 30 seconds until mustard seeds begin to pop. Immediately add onions and reduce temperature to medium. When the onion is transparent, add green chilies and sauté for a few seconds. Add coconut and continue to sauté for a minute more; add turmeric, cumin and salt and sauté for a minute. Add broccoli or spinach and continue to sauté until water is absorbed. Do not overcook the vegetable.

The recipe works well with fresh cabbage also. For ease, you may use ready-made coleslaw mixture.

Eggplant and Onion Delight

For Eggplant

1 medium purple eggplant, cut in small cubes with peel
2 tablespoons olive oil
1 teaspoon salt (or to taste)
¼ teaspoon black pepper
¹/₈ teaspoon cayenne pepper
½ teaspoon ground pomegranate seeds (anardana)

For Onion

2 medium yellow onions, sliced lengthwise
1 tablespoon olive oil
1 teaspoon salt
½ teaspoon black pepper
¼ teaspoon cayenne pepper
½ teaspoon ground pomegranate seeds (anardana)

Heat oil in skillet and add eggplant cubes. Sauté for about 10 minutes. Add salt, black pepper, cayenne, and ground pomegranate seeds. Cook eggplant cubes until done but retain their shape. Remove from skillet and keep aside, wiping skillet with paper towels. Heat 1 tablespoon oil in the same skillet, add onions & cook for 2 minutes. Add salt, black pepper, cayenne and ground pomegranate seeds & seasoning for onions. Stir and cook for 6 to 7 minutes till onions are done and transparent but not brown. Add eggplant and mix the two gently. Put in a serving dish and garnish with some sliced red tomatoes. Serves 4. Serve as a side dish with Tandoori chicken, as appetizer with crackers or sliced French bread. Traditionally, in Punjab, it is served with roti and dal made with urad and chana.

Baingan Bhurtha *(Eggplant Casserole)*

1 eggplant, roasted, peeled and mashed
2-inch piece of ginger, peeled
2 hot green chili peppers
1 large onion, peeled
2 tablespoons plus 1 teaspoon oil
1 can (15 ounce) diced tomatoes
1 teaspoon cumin seeds
1 teaspoon ground cumin
1 teaspoon coriander powder
1 teaspoon salt
1 teaspoon mango powder (amchur), optional
8 ounces frozen green peas
½ cup water or cream
Chopped fresh cilantro for garnish

In a food processor, chop ginger and hot chili peppers. Add onions and chop coarsely. Heat a large skillet, add 2 tablespoons of oil and when hot, add onion- ginger mixture and tomatoes. Cover the skillet, lower heat to medium and cook for 5-8 minutes. Uncover skillet, stir the onion mixture, push to one side of the pan & add remaining oil. Sprinkle in the cumin seeds and roast for 1 minute. Mix onion mixture with cumin. Add all other spices, peas and eggplant. Stir to mix well and cook for 3-5 minutes. Add ½ cup water or cream, cover and simmer until all liquid is absorbed. Garnish with cilantro and serve as a dry vegetable dish (sabzi).

Eggplant can be roasted in the oven, over a gas or electric stovetop or a barbeque grill. Pierce the skin with a sharp knife or skewer in several places. For oven roasting, place on a cookie sheet and cook at 400°F for 20 to 25 minutes.

Gobhi Musalam

1 head cauliflower (6 inches in diameter)
1 tablespoon Worcestershire sauce
2 teaspoons salt, or to taste
1 teaspoon black pepper, or to taste
1 teaspoon cayenne pepper
4 tablespoon olive oil, divided
1 teaspoon cumin seeds
1 tablespoon peeled and finely chopped fresh ginger,
2 cloves garlic, minced
1 medium yellow onion, sliced
1 tablespoon chopped jalapeno pepper
1 medium red tomato cut into 16 pieces
½ teaspoon turmeric
1 teaspoon paprika
2 tablespoons chopped cilantro
1 teaspoon garam masala

Remove most of the hard leaves and cut off the hard part of the stem. Wash the whole cauliflower under running water. Make a deep cross cut across the head of the cauliflower, taking care not to cut through. Sprinkle Worcestershire sauce, salt, black peppers, cayenne peppers and 1 tablespoon olive oil on the cauliflower and marinate for 1 to 2 hours. Place in a round microwavable dish. Cover and microwave on high heat for 10 minutes. Prepare masala while the cauliflower is cooking. In a small sauté pan heat 3 tablespoons oil over low to medium heat. Add cumin seeds and let crackle, add ginger, cook for 30 seconds, add garlic and cook for 10 seconds, add onion and sauté until golden brown, add turmeric, jalapeno pepper and tomatoes. Cook for 1 minute. Remove from heat and add paprika, let stand for 1 minute and add 1 tablespoon chopped cilantro. Stir and pour over cooked cauliflower. Sprinkle garam masala and the remaining cilantro. Serves 8.

Curried Kashmiri Green Apples

In Kashmir, quinces were used to prepare this delightful dish. However, Granny Smith apples may be used with equally good results. This dish is simple to prepare and may be served with a non-vegetarian or vegetarian, Western or Indian dinner.

4 hard, good sized green tart Granny Smith apples
4 tablespoons vegetable oil (canola, olive, corn is ok)
1/8 teaspoon asafetida (hing)
3-4 whole dried red chilies
1/2 teaspoon ground fennel seeds
3/4 to 1 teaspoon salt
1/4 teaspoon turmeric
1/4 teaspoon cayenne
1/4 cup water, plus extra if needed
Paprika to garnish

Wash, core and cut apples in 1/2 inch thick slices. In a 10-12 inch non-stick skillet, add oil and heat over medium heat. Add asafetida, and whole red peppers, watch these turn dark red to brown, and then add apple slices. Sauté until light brown in color. In a small bowl, mix the ground fennel, salt, turmeric, and cayenne pepper with about 1/4 cup of water. Add this spice paste to the apples and turn lightly until apples are coated. Cook on medium to low heat covered until apples are cooked (about 10 minutes). If the apples are getting dry and sticking to the skillet, add some water. Cooked apples need to be in a sauce like consistency. Remove from stove and serve in a platter. Sprinkle paprika or garnish with something red. Serves 4-6.

Green Beans Talasani (Green Beans with Garlic)

This is a quick and flavored vegetable stir-fry from the Saraswats in South India. Keep the peppers whole to retain the flavor without being hot.

1 pound frozen or fresh green beans
1 tablespoon vegetable or olive oil
4 large cloves garlic-cut in half
4 dried red hot peppers, kept whole
1 teaspoon salt
Pinch of sugar

Partially cook the beans in a microwave according to package directions & drain. If using fresh beans, remove the ends and break into 1-inch pieces. In a 2-quart wok or skillet, heat oil over medium heat. Add garlic and sauté for 1 minute. Add red peppers and cook on low until garlic is caramelized for about 1 to 2 minutes. Add beans, salt and a pinch of sugar. Sauté for 5 minutes to blend flavors and beans are cooked. Serves 6. Total cooking time 15 minutes.

You can substitute sliced zucchini, yellow squash, broccoli, tindora (small gherkins) for the beans.

Jeera Aloo Subzi (Cumin Potatoes)

1 pound potatoes, boiled, peeled and cut into ½ inch cubes
2 tablespoons vegetable oil
½ teaspoon mustard seeds
½ teaspoon cumin seeds
6-8 kari leaves
1 green pepper, finely chopped
2 teaspoons chana masala (available in Indian grocery stores)
¼ teaspoon mango powder (amchur)
¾-1 teaspoon salt (or to taste)
Pepper to taste
1 teaspoon butter

Heat oil in a deep skillet, over moderate heat. Add mustard seeds. When the mustard seeds begin to pop, add cumin seeds, kari leaves and chopped Serrano pepper. Stir and lower the heat. Add potatoes, channa masala, mango powder, salt, pepper, mix well. Cook for 3-5 minutes so that the potatoes absorb the flavor of the spices. Add butter, mix again and serve hot.

Hariyali Kofta

For Koftas

2 cups frozen green peas, thawed
3 teaspoons coriander/cumin powder
½ teaspoon turmeric powder
½ teaspoon cayenne powder
2 Serrano or hot cayenne peppers, chopped
2 tablespoons fresh ginger, grated
2 teaspoon garlic, minced
¼ cup cashews, coarsely chopped
2 teaspoons garam masala
¼ cup chickpea flour (besan)
1 ½ teaspoon salt
¼ cup golden raisins (optional)

For Gravy

2 tablespoons oil
1 cinnamon stick
5-6 black peppercorns
2 bay leaves
2 bunches green onions, chopped, tops included
2 teaspoons coriander/cumin powder mixture
1 ¼ teaspoon salt
½ teaspoon turmeric
1 teaspoon cayenne pepper
½ teaspoon garam masala
2 cups tomato puree
¼ cup water
¼ cup whipping cream
Vegetable oil for frying

Koftas

Use a food processor to mince peas (Do not over process). Pea mixture should be chunky. Add & mix all the remaining ingredients. Make 1-2 inch oval shaped balls and deep fry at 325°F until golden brown. Drain on paper towels.

Gravy

Heat oil in a non-stick saucepan over moderate heat. Add cinnamon, black peppercorns, and bay leaves. Stir for about 1 minute, then add onions. Fry until onions are soft and caramel colored, for about 5-7 minutes. Add spices, stir and then add tomato puree and water. Cook for about 15 minutes on simmer. Gravy should be thick and smooth. Add cream and heat. Add koftas to hot gravy 10 minutes prior to serving. Serve garnished with cilantro.

Kaddu Sabji *(Curried Pumpkin)*

Kaddu or pumpkin is not a vegetable you often find on the menus of Indian restaurants. In fact, one may not have eaten it except in a pumpkin pie. This unusual dish can be served even at parties!

2 pounds pie pumpkin, peel and cut into 1 inch by 1 inch by ¼ inch thick pieces
3 tablespoons vegetable oil
½ teaspoon cumin seeds
½ teaspoon fenugreek (methi) seeds
2 hot green chili peppers, chopped
2 tablespoons fresh ginger, peeled and finely chopped
½ cup raw cashews
½ cup golden raisins
½ teaspoon turmeric
2 teaspoons coriander powder
1-2 teaspoons salt
1 teaspoon sugar
2 teaspoons mango powder (amchur)
½-1 teaspoon garam masala
2 tablespoons chopped cilantro to garnish

In a wok or *kadhai*, heat oil on moderate high heat for a minute. Add cumin seeds, after 15 seconds add fenugreek seeds (methi), chopped green chilies and ginger and stir for 30 seconds. Reduce heat to low. Add cashews and fry until pale golden, add raisins and fry for 30 seconds, taking care not to burn them. Add turmeric and coriander powder and stir. Add chopped pumpkin and sprinkle salt. Stir fry to coat vegetables with spices, cover and cook for 10 to15 minutes until the vegetable is soft but not a mash. Add sugar, mango powder (amchur) and garam masala. Cook for a couple of minutes. Garnish with chopped cilantro and serve.

Cutting and peeling the skin is done much more easily if you microwave the pumpkin for a few minutes prior to cutting. Using the Swiss peeler works very well as it removes a thicker skin. Serve with puris made with addition of potatoes to the dough. You can substitute acorn squash.

Karhai Paneer (Spiced Cheese)

2 tablespoons oil
1-inch stick cinnamon
2 cloves
2 whole dried red peppers
1 bay leaf
1 red onion, sliced
1 teaspoon salt
½ teaspoon red pepper
½ cup tomato puree
½ cup water
1 package paneer (12 ounces), cubed
1 teaspoon garam masala

Put oil in a microwave safe dish. Add cinnamon, cloves, red peppers and bay leaf and microwave on high setting for 2 to 3 minutes. Add onions and cook covered for 3 to 4 minutes until onions are wilted. Add salt, red pepper, tomato puree and water. Cook for 3 to 5 minutes. Stir in the cubed paneer pieces. Add garam masala and cook covered on high for 3 to 5 minutes. Garnish with chopped cilantro and serve with roti or naan.

Batata "Song" (Saraswat Potato Curry)

The combination of potatoes (bland), onions (sweet), fenugreek (bitter), coriander (lemony), cayenne (hot), tamarind (sour) and salt provides a perfect blend of flavors. Taste the final dish and make adjustments to suit your palate. I don't know why the dish is called a "song"!

2 pounds red potatoes, boiled, peeled and cubed into 1 inch pieces (4 cups)
1 pound onions, chopped (2 cups)
5 tablespoons oil (¼ cup)
½ teaspoon fenugreek (methi) seeds, dry roasted and powdered
2 teaspoons coriander powder, dry roasted
1 teaspoon cayenne pepper
2 to 2½ teaspoons salt
Tamarind pulp from a 3-inch piece of tamarind or 2 teaspoons pulp
½ cup water or more

In a medium saucepan heat oil over medium-high heat and add onions. Sauté until pink and not brown. Add fenugreek, coriander, cayenne and then potatoes. Stir, add tamarind pulp and ½ cup of water. Cover and simmer for about 10 minutes. The onions make a thick sauce that is spicy hot, sour and slightly sweet. Serve with puris. Serves 6.

Masaledar Tofu (Curried Tofu)

Tofu is becoming increasingly popular in the Indian cuisine. It often replaces paneer or eggs in recipes. It will absorb the flavor of any curry it is added to. This high protein, low calorie dish has been very popular even with teenagers!

12 ounces extra firm tofu, mashed
2 teaspoons olive or vegetable oil, or butter
1 large onion, chopped
1 teaspoon cumin seeds
2 medium tomatoes, finely chopped
1 teaspoon minced fresh ginger
½ teaspoon minced garlic
2 hot green chili peppers, finely chopped
1 teaspoon turmeric
1 teaspoon chaat masala (available in Indian stores)
1 teaspoon salt
2 tablespoons nonfat plain yogurt
2 tablespoons chopped cilantro

In a medium nonstick pan, heat oil and sauté onions until light brown. Add cumin seeds and cook for 30 seconds. Add tomatoes, ginger, garlic, green chilies, turmeric, chaat masala and salt. Stir well and add mashed tofu and nonfat yogurt. Cook uncovered on medium heat for 10 minutes stirring occasionally. Scrape with a spatula to keep it from sticking to the bottom of the pan. Garnish with fresh chopped cilantro and serve.

Serve hot with bread or crackers. Serves 6.

Matar Paneer *(Peas and Cheese Cubes)*

1 medium onion, chopped
1-inch piece fresh ginger, peeled
3 cloves garlic
1 large or two small tomatoes
2 tablespoons oil or ghee
1 teaspoon cumin seed
¼ cup cashew pieces
¼ cup tomato sauce
2 tablespoons plain yogurt, whisked
1 teaspoon turmeric
1 ½ teaspoon salt
2 teaspoon coriander powder
½ to 1 teaspoon cayenne pepper
2 cups frozen green peas
2 cups water
1½ cup paneer cubes
1 teaspoon garam masala
Few fresh cilantro leaves, chopped

Grind onion, ginger and garlic to a smooth consistency. Separately, grind the tomatoes. In a medium saucepan, over medium heat, cook cumin seeds in oil. Add cashews and when golden, add onion mixture. Cook for a few minutes, add tomatoes and sauce. Stir and cook until oil separates from the paste. Add yogurt, stir and add all spices except garam masala. Mix well and add peas (best to thaw peas in warm water, wash and drain). Add water, stir and cook for 10 minutes on medium heat. Put paneer cubes in hot water for 2-3 minutes to soften. Drain, rinse and add to pea mixture. Reduce heat to low and cook for 5 minutes. Add garam masala, mix well and garnish with freshly chopped cilantro to serve. For a touch of sweet, add a handful of raisins while cooking. Serve 4 pieces of paneer per person. Serves 6-8.

Palak Paneer (Spinach and Cheese)

1 (12 ounce) package fresh spinach, or
10 ounces frozen spinach
1 medium onion, chopped
1 or 2 hot green chili peppers, chopped
1-inch piece fresh ginger, shredded;
divided
1¼ teaspoons salt
1 cup water
2-3 tablespoons oil or butter
1 teaspoon coriander powder
½ teaspoon black pepper
¼ cup ricotta cheese
½ cup heavy cream or 1 (12ounce) can
non-fat evaporated milk
6-8 ounces paneer cubes
½ tsp ginger, shredded
1 teaspoon garam masala

Cook spinach, onion, hot pepper, salt and half of the ginger with water for about 20 minutes. Using a hand blender, puree the mixture. I like to leave a few chunks in the mix.

Heat oil in a saucepan; add coriander powder, black pepper, ricotta cheese, and pureed spinach. Mix and sauté for 10 minutes. At this stage, the mixture tends to splatter. Add milk or cream and paneer cubes, cover and cook on low heat for 10 to 15 minutes.

Garnish with ginger shreds and garam masala. Serve with naan or roti.

Panch-Mela Saag (Five Vegetable Medley)

2 potatoes
2 sweet potatoes
1 eggplant
12-15 green beans (1/4 pound)
4 zucchini
3-4 tomatoes
1 ½ onions, chopped fine
4 tablespoons oil
6-8 kari leaves
2 tablespoons fennel seeds (saunf)
4-5 fenugreek (methi) seeds
2 tablespoons coriander powder
1 tablespoons cumin powder
1 teaspoon turmeric
1 teaspoon cayenne pepper
2 teaspoons salt (or to taste)
2 tablespoons cilantro, chopped
1/2 teaspoon garam masala (optional)

Peel and chop the vegetables except onions, into bite sized pieces.

In a medium saucepan, heat oil over moderate heat. Add kari leaves, fennel seeds (saunf), and fenugreek (methi) seeds. Wait until the seeds turn dark (about 15 seconds). Add onions and sauté for 3 4 minutes on medium heat. Lower heat and add vegetables in order of the time they take to cook (potatoes, sweet potatoes, eggplants, green beans, zucchini, tomatoes). After the addition of potatoes, sauté for 20 seconds, add 1/4 cup of water and add each vegetable after an interval of 2-3 minutes. Add coriander powder, cumin powder, turmeric and cayenne pepper. Once the vegetables are half cooked, add salt to taste. Cover and cook until vegetables are done. Garnish with cilantro and garam masala if desired. Serves 8.

Tava Mushrooms (Griddle Mushrooms)

1 pound mushrooms, washed and sliced
1 teaspoon almonds
1 teaspoon cashews
½ teaspoon poppy seeds (khus-khus)
2 tablespoons oil
1 medium onion, chopped
1 teaspoon ginger-garlic paste
1 tablespoon tomato puree
½ teaspoon salt
½ teaspoon cayenne pepper
½ cup water

Soak almonds, cashews and poppy seeds in a small amount of water. Grind to a paste. In a medium skillet heat oil, sauté onions and grind to a paste. Return to the skillet and add the grounds nuts and sauté for 1 minute. Add ginger-garlic paste and tomato puree. Stir fry to mix well. Add salt, pepper, mushrooms and water, mix, cover and cook for 10 minutes. The vegetable will be dry and oil would have separated from the vegetables. Adjust salt and pepper to taste. Serve with toasted bread, steamed rice or chapatis.

Palak Aloo *(Potatoes with Spinach)*

Spinach is a good source of iron. This vegetable side dish goes well with almost anything. The red potatoes look pretty with the green of the spinach. The spinach does not have to be completely thawed prior to cooking.

3 pounds red potatoes washed, scrubbed, and cubed
3 tablespoons oil
1 ½ teaspoons cumin seeds
1 ½ pounds frozen spinach
½ teaspoon turmeric
1 ½ teaspoons cayenne pepper
4 teaspoons coriander seeds, ground
4 teaspoons salt or to taste

Heat oil in a skillet and add cumin seeds. Let this sizzle and brown. Add potatoes, and 4 spices (salt, turmeric, chilli, and coriander). Mix well (spinach will still be frozen). Cover and cook on medium-low, about 15 to 20 minutes. Stir occasionally to prevent sticking. When potatoes are done, remove cover and cook for two minutes to let the water evaporate. Serves 8-12.

Variation

2 to 4 tablespoons dried fenugreek leaves (kasuri methi), soaked in a little water may be added along with spinach for a different flavor.

Rasedar Saunf Aloo *(Anise Flavored Potatoes in Gravy)*

This is a typical dish from Uttar Pradesh with the distinctive flavor of saunf or anise, complimenting the coriander. I knew the recipe was a success when my mother in law, who is a wonderful cook, would ask me to make it. Russet potatoes work well as they are softer and make a better gravy. If using red potatoes, mash a few potato pieces to thicken the gravy.

1¼ pounds potatoes (4 medium-large)
2 tablespoons vegetable oil
Pinch of asafetida (hing)
½ teaspoon cumin seeds
2-3 teaspoons coriander powder
1½ -2 teaspoons fennel seeds, coarsely powdered
¼ teaspoon turmeric
¼ teaspoon cayenne pepper
1½ -2 teaspoons salt
½ teaspoon mango powder (amchur)
2½ cups hot water

Boil potatoes until tender. Cool, peel and cube into ½ inch pieces. In a 2-quart saucepan, heat oil over medium heat. Add asafetida (hing). Add cumin seeds and sauté for 30 seconds until they change color. Add coriander, fennel, turmeric and cayenne. Stir for a few seconds, taking care not to burn spices. Add potatoes and sauté for 5 minutes. Add hot water and simmer for 10 minutes. Serve with hot puris, mint (pudina) raita and mango pickle for a wonderful brunch. Makes 1 quart & serves 4.

During religious functions, many Indians do not eat garlic or onion. This recipe works well for such occasions as it can easily be multiplied and is easy to make. Served with just puris and raita, a 5-pound bag of potatoes serves 15 and a 10-pound bag of potatoes makes enough for 30 people. Use a 6-quart or 12-quart heavy bottomed pot.

Saffron Corn

Another award winning recipe from the International cooking competition held in Baton Rouge, Louisiana. A microwave to cook the corn and food processor to grind ingredients shortens cooking time.

2 cups frozen corn kernels
3 corn on the cob, cut into 1½- inch pieces
2 medium onions
1 teaspoon ginger, minced
5 cloves garlic
4 teaspoons oil
1½ teaspoon garam masala
½ teaspoon turmeric
½ teaspoon cayenne pepper
1 (8 oz) can tomato sauce
2 pinches saffron
1 teaspoon cilantro, chopped
1 tablespoon heavy cream
1½ teaspoons salt, to taste

Cook corn on the cobs until tender in a pot or pressure cooker. Cook frozen corn kernels and mix the two. Grind onion, ginger and garlic to a paste. In a medium saucepan, heat oil and sauté the paste over medium heat until it turns golden brown. Add garam masala, turmeric, cayenne pepper & mix well. Add tomato sauce and corn mixture and simmer for 7-8 minutes over medium heat. Soak saffron in a 1 tablespoonful of warm water for 15 minutes. Add saffron-water mixture to corn mixture and mix well. Garnish with cilantro and heavy cream. Serve hot over rice or chapati.

Soy Aloo Matar (Soy, Potatoes and Peas)

Soybeans are becoming more popular these days because of their health benefits. Fresh frozen beans, soymilk, roasted soy nuts, soybean flour and packets of small and large nuggets are easily available. For the vegetarians this is a good source of protein and the nuggets absorb the flavor of the curry and the texture becomes similar to meat or ground meat.

1 tablespoon oil
1 cup soy nuggets
1 recipe Punjabi Masala*
1 medium potato, peeled and cubed
1 cup frozen green peas, thawed
1 teaspoon salt
2-3 cups warm water
2 tablespoons chopped fresh cilantro, for garnish

Heat oil in a saucepan. Add soy nuggets and sauté until lightly brown. Remove and drain on a paper towel. Add masala to the pan along with potatoes, peas and salt. Stir to coat all the vegetables with masala. Cook for 3-5 minutes. Add warm water and bring to boil. Cover and simmer for 15 minutes or until potatoes are tender. Adjust salt and pepper. Sometimes the nuggets absorb all the gravy, so you may need to add more liquid.

Garnish with cilantro and serve with rice or roti. Serves 4

See page 221 for Punjabi Masala. Soy nuggets can be purchased from an Indian grocery store.

Spiced Cabbage with Potatoes

2 tablespoons vegetable oil
¼ teaspoon mustard seeds
4 medium potatoes, diced
1 head fresh cabbage (washed and shredded fine)
½ teaspoon turmeric
½ teaspoon cumin powder
½ teaspoon coriander powder
½ teaspoon paprika
Pinch of sugar
1 teaspoon salt or more to taste
2 tomatoes, fresh (chopped) or canned
1 cup green peas
¼ teaspoon ginger root (mashed or grated)
½ teaspoon garam masala

Heat oil in a sauté pan over medium heat & add mustard seeds. Cook for 30 seconds until they begin to pop. Add potatoes and sauté and add cabbage. Stir to coat the mixture well with oil. Add turmeric, cumin, coriander powder, paprika, sugar, salt and tomatoes while stirring. (When cabbage is not fresh sprinkle a little water). As the mixture becomes moist, add peas, lower the heat, cover & simmer for 5-8 minutes. Turn the heat off when potatoes are tender. Add ginger and garam masala for flavor.

Bharele Baingan Aloo *(Eggplant Gujarati)*

Gujarat State in western India is a predominantly vegetarian State. Peanuts are liberally used in vegetables and salads. Unlike other regions, coriander and cumin are used together in a mixed powder form.

1 cup chickpea flour (besan)
½ cup coriander-cumin powder mix
¼ cup peanuts, coarsely ground
1 teaspoon turmeric
2 teaspoons cayenne pepper
2 teaspoons salt or to taste
½ cup fresh cilantro, chopped
1 pound small fresh red potatoes, peeled
1 pound small or baby eggplant (baingan)
1 large onion, sliced thick
1 cup vegetable oil
2 teaspoons mustard seeds
Pinch of asafetida (hing)

Mix chickpea flour, coriander-cumin powder, peanuts, turmeric, cayenne, salt and chopped cilantro in a bowl. This is the masala or stuffing. Make a cross-slit in the potatoes and eggplant such that the ends remain together. Stuff the openings with masala and set aside. Heat oil in a large skillet. Add mustard seeds and asafetida. When mustard seeds begin to pop add potatoes. Stir gently to coat them with oil; taking care not to lose the masala. Cook for 15 minutes on medium heat to give the potatoes a head start. Add eggplant, onions and any leftover masala and mix to coat the vegetables. Cover and continue to cook for another 15 to 20 minutes, stirring occasionally to prevent sticking and burning. Cook until the potatoes are soft.

Dhania-jeera (coriander-cumin) powder mix is available at the Indian grocery stores. The proportion of coriander to cumin varies with different brands and individuals. One can use 3:1 or 2:1 ratio of coriander to cumin.

Bharwan Bhindi (Okra)

Stuffed Okra

1 pound baby okra
½ cup chickpea (besan) flour
1 ½ teaspoons garam masala
1 teaspoon salt
½ teaspoon cayenne pepper
¼ teaspoon turmeric
1 cup cilantro (loosely packed) & chopped
½ cup plus 1 tablespoon vegetable oil
½ teaspoon cumin seeds
½ teaspoon mustard seeds

Wash and remove both ends of okra. Make slit in the okra (for stuffing).

To the besan add garam masala, salt, cayenne pepper & turmeric .Add cilantro and 1 tablespoon oil and mix all the ingredients well. Divide the mixture into two equal portions

Stuffing and cooking okra

Using half of the stuffing mix, stuff each okra loosely. In a large sauté pan, heat ½ cup oil over medium heat and add cumin and mustard seeds. Cook for 15 seconds till the mustard seeds begin to pop. Add stuffed okra and stir gently to coat thoroughly with oil. Cover the pan and cook on low to medium heat stirring occasionally until okra is tender. Sprinkle the remaining stuffing mix evenly and stir gently. Continue cooking uncovered until okra is golden brown.

Bharwan Karela (Bitter Gourd)

8 bitter gourds (karelas)
¼ cup oil
2 tablespoons oil
1 cup sliced onions
1 tablespoon karela masala
(refer masala section)

For Filling

1 large yellow onion
2 hot green reen peppers
(Cayenne, Jalapeno or Thai)
4 cloves garlic
1 cubic inch fresh ginger
3 tablespoons karela masala
¼ cup oil
1 teaspoon cumin seeds
¼ cup white vinegar

Scrape karelas ridges with a peeler and save the peel. Cut into 3-inch long cylinders. Make a slit, cutting up to the center and not all the way. Sprinkle salt & turmeric mixture and set in a colander to drain for 30 minutes. Spread karelas in single layer on a kitchen towel, place in the sun for 1 hour, or in a 200°F oven for 45 minutes to partially dehydrate.

For the Filling

Puree onions, hot pepper, garlic and ginger in a food processor. Heat oil, add cumin seeds and quickly add pureed onion mixture. Cook on medium heat until onions turn brown and oil separates. Add karela masala and cook for 30 seconds, stiring continuously. Add vinegar and cook for 30 more seconds. The mixture will be moist, not runny.

Stuff karelas with the filling and tie with a string to secure filling.

Heat oil in a flat wide skillet, on medium heat. Pan fry karelas in a single layer. Cook until karelas are evenly browned on all sides. You may partially cook on stovetop and then in 350°F oven for 30-45 minutes, turning frequently. Do not cover during cooking or after until cooled completely. Transfer to a serving platter. In the same pan, heat 2 tablespoons oil, cook sliced onions until wilted. Sprinkle one tablespoon karela masala on the onions. Spread onions on top of the karelas and serve hot or cold. Serves 8-12.

Bharwan Tori *(Stuffed Zucchini)*

This is an excellent dish for advance preparation. Simply heat and serve then enjoy the gourmet complements.

8 medium zucchini

For Stuffing

2 tablespoons oil
1 teaspoon cumin seed
1 tablespoon ginger, thinly sliced
1 tablespoon garlic, chopped
1 cup onion, chopped
½ cup green onion, chopped
2-3 bay leaves
2 teaspoons jalapeno pepper, chopped
1 teaspoon turmeric
1 pound ground pork
1 teaspoon salt
1 tablespoon tomato paste
2 teaspoon paprika
1 tablespoon bulgur wheat
1 teaspoon sugar
¼ cup chopped cilantro
1 teaspoon garam masala
¼ teaspoon seeds from black cardamoms, crushed
½ cup sliced onions, marinated for 10 minutes in 2 tablespoons salad vinegar and sprinkle of salt
Ice cold water

Cut zucchini in 2- inch long drums. Scrape out the pulp and hollow the zucchini pieces with a paring knife, leaving hollow cylinders with walls intact. Cook zucchini in boiling water for 3 minutes. Transfer immediately into ice-cold water to stop further cooking. Drain in a colander. Set zucchini on a baking tray.

Stuffing

Heat oil in a heavy bottomed skillet, over moderate heat. Add cumin seeds & let them crackle. Add ginger & cook for 30 seconds, add garlic and cook for another 30 seconds. Add onions and sauté to light brown. Add green onions, bay leaves, jalapeno and cook until green onions wilt. Add turmeric, mix, add pork, sprinkle salt and cook pork. Stir, as needed, to prevent sticking or burning. Add tomato paste and paprika, continue to cook, until oil separates from the mixture. Add bulgur wheat and sugar and cook for 1 minute. Remove mixture into a colander to drain fat. Place meat in a food processor and process for 2-3 minutes. Add cilantro, garam masala and cardamom seeds and mix. Stuff the zucchini cylinders firmly. Set aside or refrigerate for longer storage. Before serving, preheat oven to 350 degrees F and bake zucchini for 10 minutes. Garnish with marinated onion. Serve with a meal or as an appetizer. Makes approximately 24 pieces.

Sarson Ka Saag *(Mustard Greens)*

The State of Punjab in north is the agricultural heartland of India. There are vast fields of wheat, corn and mustard and during winter months mustard greens with cornmeal tortillas (makki ki roti) are a favorite meal. Lucky for us that fresh mustard greens and hand ground cornmeal are also favorite foods in Louisiana!

2 pounds fresh, or frozen, mustard greens
2 pounds fresh, or frozen, spinach
½ stick butter or margarine
1 to 2 ounces fresh dill, chopped (optional)
1 tablespoon ginger, finely chopped
2 Jalapeno peppers, finely chopped
1 ½ to 2 teaspoons salt

For Tadka
1½ cup chopped onion
4 large cloves of garlic, chopped
½ stick (2 ounces) butter or margarine
2 tablespoons cornmeal
½ cup heavy cream
1 teaspoon garam masala
1 cup hot water

Melt butter in a 5-quart saucepan. Add mustard greens, spinach, dill, ginger, hot pepper and salt. Cook for 20 minutes over moderate heat. The mustard-spinach mixture should not be totally dry but have some liquid.

For Tadka, heat a sauté pan and melt butter. Sauté onions and garlic until golden. Then add cornmeal and stir until light brown. Add cream and cornmeal mixture to the vegetable mix (saag) along with hot water. Mix well, cover and simmer for 30 minutes. Sprinkle with garam masala before serving.

A food processor speeds up the chopping step. This saag tastes better when served the next day. Fresh mustard greens have a distinctive nutty flavor. Serve with makki ki roti or naan & yogurt lassi.

Tawa Masala Sabji (Griddle Masala Vegetables)

Masala
2 tablespoons ghee or oil
1 cup finely diced onion
1 tablespoon fresh ginger, grated
1 tablespoon fresh garlic, finely chopped
2 tablespoons tomato puree
2 tablespoons whipping cream
2 hot green chilies, finely chopped
1 teaspoon garam masala
1 teaspoon paprika
1 teaspoon salt
2 tablespoons cilantro, chopped
Cayenne pepper to taste (optional)

Vegetables
1 zucchini, sliced
6 miniature eggplants or 2 long purple ones cut into 3 pieces each
8 okra
¼ cup mushrooms
2 cups sliced onions
Oil for deep- frying

Deep fry vegetables, one kind at a time and set aside. Do not cover. Arrange vegetables on the periphery of the tawa (griddle).

Heat oil in the center of the hot tawa; sauté onion to golden brown, add ginger and garlic, cook for another minute until the preparation is golden brown. Add whipping cream and cook until cream evaporates and ghee separates from the mixture. Add chilies and mix well. Pull this prepared masala to the side of the tawa.

Arrange fried vegetables on the periphery of the tawa. Mix vegetables and enough masala to coat the vegetables. Mix all or a few servings at a time. Serve immediately.

Sukha Aloo (Dry Potatoes)

4 pounds potatoes
1 cup vegetable oil
2 tablespoons cumin powder
2 tablespoons coriander powder
2 teaspoons cayenne pepper
1 tablespoon salt, adjust to taste
1 tablespoon paprika
4 tablespoons cilantro, chopped (garnish)

Boil, peel and cut potatoes into one-inch cubes. Heat oil in a heavy bottomed pan. *Place the spices in little mounds in a platter for convenience.* Dump spices in the pan, all at the same time. Stir for a few seconds and add potato cubes. Coat well & cook for 5 minutes. Remove to a serving dish and garnish with chopped cilantro. Serve hot. Serves 20

Ankurit Moong *(Sprouted Mung Beans)*

1½ cups sabut (whole) moong
2 tablespoons oil
½ teaspoon jeera
1½ teaspoon salt
¼ teaspoon haldi
2 teaspoon coriander powder
½–¾ teaspoon cayenne pepper
2 teaspoon lemon juice
1 cup water

Wash moong in several changes of water. Soak in hot water, cover & leave overnight or for about 12 hours. Line a colander with cheesecloth and drain moong over the cloth. Fold corners of the cloth over moong. Keep in a warm place, and keep the cheesecloth moist. Moong should sprout well in 24 hours to 48 hours. In a 3-inch deep large pan, heat oil over moderate heat.. Add cumin and let it sizzle for about 30 seconds. Add ginger and chili pepper, sauté till light brown. Add moong, salt, turmeric and coriander powder. Stir for 2 to 3 minutes, add water, and give a final stir and cover. Lower heat to medium-low and cook for 15 minutes. Uncover and stir, water should be completely absorbed, moong cooked but not mushy. If not done cook another 5 minutes. Stir in lemon juice and remove from heat. Serve with rice, kadhi, any vegetable and roti. Can also be used for chaat.

Chana Dal with Mirlitons

3 tablespoons vegetable oil
2 teaspoons black mustard seeds
2 teaspoons fresh ginger, peeled and shredded
1 sliced serrano pepper
25 kari leaves
2 mirlitons peeled, deseeded and diced into 1-inch pieces
2 cups chana dal, washed and soaked in tap water for 45 minutes
½ teaspoon turmeric
½-1 teaspoon cayenne pepper
3 teaspoons salt
2 teaspoons coriander powder
3 cups water

Heat oil and add mustard seeds until they pop. Add ginger, serrano pepper and kari leaves. Stir for 20 seconds. Add mirlitons and channa dal. Stir for a minute. Add rest of the spices, stir and add water. Bring to a boil. Lower heat to medium and cook covered for 20-30 minutes. Note that mirlitons and channa dal should be soft and not mushy or cook in a pressure cooker for 15 minutes after one whistle. Serve hot. Makes 3-4 quarts.

Cuccuzza squash (lauki) or any other squash can be substituted for mirliton.

Rajmah *(Red Kidney Beans in a slow cooker)*

Red beans and rice is a traditional Monday supper in Louisiana. Mondays were wash days, and since there was no time to cook, ladies would put a pot of beans on the stove to simmer all day long. Here, the modern slow cooker accomplishes the same for the modern woman.

1 cup red beans (rajmah)
1 small bell pepper, chopped
1 small onion chopped
1 medium tomato chopped
4 cloves garlic minced
1½ teaspoons salt or to taste
½ teaspoon methi (fenugreek) seeds
½ teaspoon cumin seeds
1 teaspoon cayenne pepper or to taste
1 teaspoon garam masala
4 cups cold water
1 tablespoon fresh chopped cilantro

Place all ingredients except cilantro, in a 2 or 3-quart slow cooker. Cook on high for 5-6 hours. Sprinkle with chopped fresh cilantro before serving.

Dal Makhani

1 cup whole urad dal (sabut urad)
½ cup red kidney beans
1 tablespoon oil
1 teaspoon cumin
1 medium onion, chopped
2-inch piece fresh ginger, grated
8 cloves garlic, chopped
1 teaspoon turmeric
1 serrano pepper, finely chopped
1 teaspoon coriander powder
1 ½ teaspoons salt
1 teaspoon cayenne pepper
5 cups water
1 cup heavy cream
1 teaspoon garam masala
3-4 tablespoons butter

Wash urad dal and red beans in several changes of water and soak in 3 cups of cold water for 2 hours or more. Heat oil in a Dutch oven and add cumin seeds. When cumin has roasted for about 30 seconds, add onion, ginger and garlic. Stir-fry for 5 minutes until onions are golden brown. Add turmeric, serrano pepper, coriander powder, salt, cayenne pepper and stir to mix. Drain dal and beans and add to the pan. Mix and add 5 cups of water. Bring to a boil, cover and cook for 1-2 hours on medium-low heat. Add more water, if needed. Cook dal until some of the beans are very soft. Mash a few beans with the back of a spatula. Stir in the cream, garam masala and butter. It should be the consistency of a thick soup. Serve topped with additional amount of golden brown onions and garlic that has been slow cooked.

This dal improves in flavor when refrigerated. It is best in flavor when cooked in cast iron Dutch oven. This recipe can also be cooked in a slow cooker. Reduce water to 4 cups for slow cooker.

Dal Palak *(Mung Dal with Spinach)*

1 cup mung beans (sabut moong)
4 cups water
1 medium onion, chopped
1 medium tomato, chopped
1 teaspoon turmeric
1 teaspoon salt
1 (10-ounce) package frozen spinach, chopped
1 teaspoon minced garlic
1 teaspoon fresh ginger, chopped
2 hot green chili peppers (optional)
2 tablespoons vegetable oil or melted butter
1 teaspoon cumin seeds
1 teaspoon garam masala
½ teaspoon black pepper
2 tablespoons lemon juice

Wash moong dal well and soak for 15 minutes in 4 cups of water. Bring water to a boil in the pressure cooker (or a heavy pan) on high heat and add moong dal, chopped onions, chopped tomato, turmeric powder and salt. Close the pressure cooker and cook for 3 minutes after one whistle. Remove cooker from heat and let the pressure fall. Remove cover and add spinach, garlic, ginger and green pepper. Cook for 10 minutes on medium heat, uncovered.

Tadka: Heat butter/oil in a small non-stick pan add cumin seeds, garam masala, black pepper and lemon juice and add to dal. Serve with any bread, rice or chapati. Serves 6.

Masoor Amti *(Lentil Soup)*

1½ cup brown lentils (sabut masoor)
6-8 cups water, divided
3-4 tablespoons oil
1 medium onion, finely chopped (1 cup)
2 Roma tomatoes, chopped (1 cup)
¾ teaspoon mustard seeds
½ teaspoon turmeric
1-2 teaspoon amti powder
2 teaspoons salt
Chopped fresh cilantro for garnish

Clean and wash the lentils. Cook lentils in 6 cups of water until lentils are very soft (about 30 minutes). Alternatively pressure cook for 1 whistle and reduce the water to 4 cups. In a medium size skillet, heat oil on medium heat & add mustard seeds. When they begin to pop, add onions and cook until translucent. Add tomatoes and cook for 2-3 minutes (do not cook tomatoes to a pulp). Add turmeric and amti powder. Take pan off the heat. Add 2 cups water to lentils along with salt and bring to a boil. Add tomato-onion mixture to the lentils and cook over low heat for 10 minutes, stirring occasionally to blend the flavors.

Garnish with chopped cilantro and serve with rice or as a hot soup.

This dish can also be made in a slow cooker substituting Roma tomatos with diced canned tomatoes.
Amti powder is available through mail order.

Sambhar

3/4 cup arhar/toor dal
2 cups mixed vegetables such as eggplant, cauliflower, carrots, squash, okra, beans
8-10 curry leaves
¼ teaspoon turmeric
2 teaspoons salt
2 teaspoons tamarind paste
1 tomato, chopped
2 tablespoons sambhar powder, (preferably MTR)
1 teaspoon sugar optional

For Baghaar

1-2 tablespoon oil
½ teaspoon mustard seeds
1 teaspoon urad dal
6-7 curry leaves
½ onion, optional

Wash and soak dal in 2 cups of water for about 20 minutes. Boil dal about 15-20 minutes or 2 whistles in a pressure cooker, until soft. Let pressure drop by itself. Add turmeric, curry leaves and vegetables and boil again until vegetables are soft. Mix sambhar powder in half cup of water and add to dal along with tamarind, tomato, salt and sugar, if using. Simmer for a few more minutes.

For Baghar: Heat oil and add mustard seeds. As soon as mustard seeds begin to pop, add urad dal and curry leaves. When urad dal becomes pinkish, add onions. Sauté till translucent and add baghaar to sambhar. Check for seasoning, adding more if needed. Serve with idlis, dosas or vadas. Any sambhar powder can be substituted for MTR. Add a little at a time if using a different brand.

Sindhi Kadhi (Chickpea Flour Curry)

This curry is similar to a vegetable soup that has been thickened with a roux made of chickpea flour instead of all-purpose flour. Traditional Indian seasonings and a combination of vegetables are used. The finished dish tastes somewhat similar to sambhar (lentil and vegetable stew) from southern India.

4 tablespoons oil
1 teaspoon cumin seeds(jeera)
1 teaspoon mustard seeds (rai)
1 teaspoon fenugreek seeds (methi)
1 inch fresh ginger, peeled and chopped
1 hot Serrano chili pepper
1 cup chickpea flour (besan)
8 cups water
10-12 kari leaves
½ teaspoon crushed red pepper flakes or cayenne pepper
Vegetables of your choice (okra, potatoes, string beans, carrots, zucchini, etc).
2 tomatoes, chopped
Salt to taste
Tamarind pulp or lemon juice

In a big pot heat 4 tablespoons oil over moderate heat. Add a mixture of cumin, mustard and fenugreek seeds. Cook on high heat until you get the aroma of the spices. Add ginger, Serrano chilies and sauté for a few seconds, add besan and keep stirring for about 15 minutes or until besan is golden brown. Take care to stir constantly to prevent besan from getting burnt at the bottom. Add water and blend with besan. The curry should be neither too thick or too thin. Add kari leaves and tomatoes and continue to boil the curry. You may add tamarind concentrate or lemon juice to get a slightly sour taste. Add cut up vegetables of your choice. Please note that whole okra is preferred and should be fried before adding to the curry. You may fry all the vegetables. Boil the curry on medium heat. When the vegetables are cooked and tender, the curry is ready to be served. Serve with white rice. Sweet boondi is a traditional Sindhi dessert that is served with this meal.

The testers served it with idlis (steamed rice and lentil cakes) and coconut chutney for a wonderful new flavor.

Sookha Urad

2 cups skinless urad dal
2-3 tablespoons oil
1 teaspoon cumin seeds
½ cup red onion, finely chopped
1 teaspoon ginger, freshly grated
1 teaspoon turmeric
1 teaspoon coriander powder
¾ teaspoon salt
1 serrano chili pepper, seeded and finely chopped
½ cup red and green bell pepper, each finely chopped
1 cup water
¼ teaspoon paprika
½ teaspoon garam masala
1 tablespoon fresh cilantro, chopped
Juice of one lime
Sliced tomatoes for garnish

Wash dal in several changes of water and soak in 3 cups of cold water for 2 hours or more. Heat oil in a sauté pan and add cumin. When cumin has roasted for about 30 seconds, add ½ of the onion and ginger and stir-fry for a minute. Add turmeric, coriander & salt and stir to mix. Drain dal and add to the pan. Mix, and add Serrano pepper, ½ of the bell pepper and ½ of water. Cover the pan and cook for ten minutes.

Add more water, if needed. Cook dal to 'al-dente' stage. Stir in the limejuice, paprika, chopped cilantro and remaining onions and bell pepper. Cover and let it sit for 5 minutes, prior to transferring it to a serving platter. Garnish with sliced tomatoes (optional).

Egg Curry

Meats and Seafood

Keema Matar *(Ground Meat and Peas)*

Keema Matar, a versatile and jiffy preparation of authentic Indian taste, resembles Mexican chili con carne. Use it to make Sloppy Joes, Tacos, on pizza or stuffing for calzones or meat pies etc, even on pasta. It combines well with cheese and raw onion-tomato salad. It is so easy and delicious!

1 pound ground chicken or turkey
1 pound ground pork
1 tablespoon oil, if needed
1 medium coarsely diced yellow onion
2 or 3 chopped green onions, all parts
1 teaspoon grated fresh ginger, optional
1 teaspoon garlic, crushed
1 tablespoon hot green pepper finely chopped or to taste
2 tablespoons tomato paste
2 teaspoons salt or to taste
1 teaspoon cumin seeds
1 teaspoon cumin powder
1 teaspoon cayenne pepper
2 teaspoons paprika
¼ cup water or more as wanted
1 cup frozen peas, thawed under running warm water.
¼ cup chopped cilantro

Place a heavy-bottomed skillet on medium heat. When skillet is hot crumble ground meat in a single layer and turn frequently to prevent sticking until redness disappears completely. Add oil if the mixture seems to be too dry. Add the next five ingredients and continue to cook on medium heat for 10 more minutes until all the fresh ingredients soften. Make a well in the center of the meat mixture and put tomato paste in the center of the well. Stir rapidly for 30 seconds and then mix with the rest. Add the next 5 ingredients, all at one time, mix well, cook for 1 minute and add water. Cover and cook for 5 minutes. Add thawed peas and cook until peas are soft but still green. Add cilantro. Keema Mattar is ready to be served with chapati, parathas or rice. Keep Keema Matar thick or add water to bring to the desired consistency for the intended use.

Bhuna Kaleji (Goa Chicken Liver)

Chicken liver is easy to cook and a good source of iron. Surprisingly the two souring agents, vinegar as well as tamarind, does not make the dish sour, but tamarind adds a sweet taste to the dish. Use of vinegar in cooking is a Portugese influence. Goa, on the West Coast of India was a Portuguese colony until 1960.

2 pounds chicken liver
1 large onion chopped coarsely
4 large cloves garlic chopped
2 tablespoons ginger, peeled and grated
1 serrano or other hot chili pepper, with seeds
4 tablespoons vegetable oil
1 teaspoon turmeric
½ teaspoon cayenne pepper
1 level teaspoon tamarind concentrate or 2 teaspoons tamarind pulp
1 ½ teaspoons salt
¼ teaspoon freshly ground black pepper
2 tablespoons vinegar

Remove veins and any fat around the liver. Separate the lobes. Rinse the liver and drain. Grind onions, ginger, garlic and serrano pepper with vinegar to a smooth paste. Mix the liver pieces and coat well. Heat oil in a 10 or 12-inch nonstick pan over moderate heat. Add liver and turmeric, cayenne pepper and black pepper. Shallow fry on moderately high heat, stirring often. When slightly dry, add salt and tamarind pulp and mix well. Cook till liver is well cooked and dry. Serve either with parathas or rolled in flour tortillas. Also makes a good filling between 2 slices of bread. To reheat, warm in the microwave on low.

Chennai Chicken *(Chicken South Indian)*

This chicken curry comes from Chennai, formerly Madras. India's Southern States use more cayenne than the rest of India. The heat in this recipe has been toned down to suit changing tastes without compromising the flavor.

2 pounds boneless chicken breast, cut into 1 to 2-inch pieces
2 onions, chopped
1 can (15 ounce) tomatoes, diced
3 tablespoons oil
4-5 teaspoons chana dal
2-3 whole dried red chilli peppers
1 teaspoon coriander seeds
1 teaspoon cumin seeds
¼ cup grated coconut, fresh or frozen
2 tablespoons minced ginger
6-8 cloves garlic, minced
½ teaspoon cayenne pepper
1 teaspoon turmeric
2 cups warm water
1 ½ teaspoons salt or to taste
1 tablespoon cilantro or Kari leaves, chopped

Heat a non-stick skillet, add 1 tablespoon oil, and add chana dal, dry chili peppers, coriander and cumin seeds. Roast for a few minutes; add coconut, garlic and ginger. Cook for 2 minutes. Remove from heat, and grind into a paste. Heat remaining oil in a Dutch oven and sauté onions until golden brown. Add ground paste and sauté for 2 to 3 minutes. Add tomatoes, cayenne pepper and turmeric, then chicken. Stir together. Add water, cover and cook on low heat until the chicken is done or for about 30 minutes. Garnish with cilantro, and Kari Patta. Serve with plain rice. Serves 4.

Chicken Kabab *(Murgh Kabab)*

2 pounds boneless chicken breast
¼ cup garlic cloves
¼ cup red wine vinegar
1 tablespoon coriander powder
2 teaspoons salt
2 teaspoons paprika
1 teaspoon cayenne pepper
1 teaspoon dried ginger powder (sonth)
¼ cup vegetable oil
Garnish and enhancer
1 tablespoon chopped cilantro
¼ cup sliced onion
1 tablespoon fresh lemon juice

Wash and cut chicken in 1½- inch cubes & place in a deep bowl. Blend all other ingredients in a blender. Pour over the chicken & coat pieces thoroughly. Marinate for 8 hours, preferaly overnight, in the refrigerator. Preheat oven to broil or heat BBQ grill on high. Lace the pieces onto bamboo skewers and barbeque or broil for 5 minutes on one side. Turn over and cook for 5 more minutes. Do not over cook as chicken will turn tough and dry. Garnish with cilantro and sliced onions. Sprinkle fresh lemon juice just before serving. Serve with lemon rice. Serves 8.

Suggestions: May alternate bell pepper and onions in the skewers.

Easy Chicken

This very simple recipe comes from the southern most State of Kerala. Liberal use of kari leaves gives it an unique flavor. Fiery hot food is characteristic of southern cuisine. Experiment with the amount of cayenne pepper you use!

4 tablespoons vegetable oil
20-25 kari leaves with stems attached
2-3 tablespoons of cayenne pepper
2 ½ pounds chicken, cut into small pieces
2 teaspoons salt, or to taste
4-5 tablespoons Maggi Tomato Sauce

In a heavy pot, sauté curry leaves in oil and cover until kari leaves are cooked (for about 1 minute). Add pepper, mix and cook until pepper aroma changes for 20 seconds. Add chicken to the kari-pepper mixture and cook chicken till nearly cooked (about 15to 20 minutes). Mix often to allow an even blend. Add salt to taste. Add tomato sauce and cook for another 5 minutes. Serve with plain rice.

Maggi brand can be found in Indian grocery stores.

Chicken Tandoori

Tandoori chicken is one of the most widely known amongst Indian dishes. It is found on the menu of most north Indian restaurants. Addition of red food coloring gives the dish its typical color seen in restaurants. Many people, however, avoid using artificial colors as this recipe also has done. The flavor here is predominantly that of cumin. This recipe was used for many, many years for the Indian Students Association banquet at Louisiana State University in Baton Rouge. Many a past student will recognize the flavor!

4 pounds chicken parts (breasts, leg and thigh, skinned)
2 tablespoons fresh ginger
2 tablespoons fresh garlic
4 ounces plain yogurt
8 ounces sour cream
2 ounces (½ cup) cumin seeds, roasted and ground
1 teaspoon cayenne pepper
1 tablespoon lemon juice
1 teaspoon paprika
Salt to taste

For Marinade

Blend all ingredients together except chicken. Cut chicken into serving size. Pour marinade over the chicken and marinate overnight. Bake chicken in a covered baking pan for 45 minutes at 350°F. Uncover and cook for additional 15 minutes. Baste a few times and turn chicken once during baking. Serve with rice, potatoes, peas, corn or salad. Serves 8.

Egg Curry

An appreciable number of vegetarians do not object to eating eggs. Therefore, eggs are a good substitute to meat and poultry. This is a spicy and appetizing preparation. An ideal dish for the South Louisiana palate!

For Egg Curry

4 eggs
4 cloves garlic,
One small piece of ginger
2 hot green chili peppers
¼ cup corn oil
2 onions, chopped
Salt to taste
Pinch of turmeric
1 tablespoon garam masala
½ teaspoon mango powder
2 bay leaves
2 tomatoes, chopped
1 can (8-ounce) tomato sauce
¼ cup plain yogurt
¼ teaspoon sugar
Chopped cilantro for garnish

For Basmati Rice

1 cup basmati (long grain) rice
1 ¾ cups water
2 tablespoons butter
4 cloves
1 stick cinnamon
½ teaspoon cumin seeds
8 whole cashew nuts
10 golden raisins
¼ cup green peas, shelled & boiled
Salt to taste

Boil eggs and peel the shell. Mince garlic, ginger and green pepper to make paste. Heat oil in a pan, lightly fry eggs on all sides. Take out and cut them in halves. Put them aside. Add chopped onions in the pan and sauté until golden brown. Add garlic/ginger/green pepper paste. Continue to sauté for 2 minutes. Add salt, turmeric, garam masala, dry mango powder and bay leaves. Sauté for 2 minutes. Add chopped tomatoes, yogurt, tomato sauce, sugar, and allow to simmer. Cook until gravy becomes thick. Add eggs. Bring to boil and simmer for 3 minutes. Garnish with chopped cilantro.

Melt butter and add cloves, cinnamon, cashews and cumin seeds. Keep aside.

Bring water to boil and add salt, and spicy melted butter. Now cook rice in this mixture.

After rice is cooked, add raisins and boiled green peas. Gently mix. Serve hot egg curry over a bed of rice. Garnish lightly with chopped cilantro. Serves 2

Lamb Chops Kashmiri Style

½ rack of lamb or loin chops
1 small onion
1 teaspoon fresh ginger, peeled
1 teaspoon garlic, minced
1 Serrano pepper, seeded
4 whole almonds
2 tablespoons plain yogurt
2-3 tablespoon oil
¼ to ½ teaspoon ground cumin
½ to 1 teaspoon coriander powder
¼ teaspoon turmeric
½ cup chopped fruit (peach, papaya or mango)
1 teaspoon salt
½ inch stick cinnamon
1 cup water
¼ cup cream
¼ teaspoon paprika
2-3 strands saffron
¼ to ½ teaspoon garam masala
1 teaspoon chopped fresh mint, or ½ teaspoon dry mint

Separate lamb chops using a sharp knife. Remove fat. Wash and pat dry. Using a food processor, grind onion, garlic, ginger, serrano pepper, almonds and yogurt into a paste. Heat a skillet large enough to hold chops in a single layer. Add oil and sauté lamb chops for 2 minutes on each side to get a good sear on the meat. Remove to a plate. Add spice paste to the hot oil in the pan and stir-fry for 3 to 4 minutes. Add cumin, coriander powder and turmeric. Mix with the paste and cook for about 2 minutes until paste is roasted and oil separates. Place lamb chops into the pan and stir to coat the chops with the paste. Add fruit, salt, cinnamon and water. Cover and simmer for 45 minutes. Uncover the pan and increase heat to evaporate most of the water. Mix saffron and paprika with cream and add to the meat. Cook until a thick sauce develops. Remove cinnamon. Add garam masala and mint. Serve 2-3 chops per person.

Lamb "Do Piaza" with Mushrooms

The name "do piazza" comes from the use of onions in two forms and two stages. It is a cooking technique, used in mughlai cooking and in this country has been adopted by Paul Prudhomme.

2 pounds boneless lamb shoulder
4-5 onions
¼ cup oil
1 ½ teaspoon panch phoran or garam masala
4 bay leaves
½ cup plain yogurt
½ cup water
¼ teaspoon turmeric
¼ teaspoon cayenne pepper
1 teaspoon salt
Pinch black pepper
½ pound fresh mushrooms, cleaned

Remove fat from the meat, cube, wash and pat dry with paper towels.

Peel onions and slice half of these into thin slices. Finely chop the remaining onions.

Heat a heavy-duty skillet or pan, add oil. Fry the sliced onions until dark. Remove with slotted spoon to a plate and set aside. In the same oil, add panch phoran and bay leaves. Sauté for 1 minute, add chopped onions and meat. Cook together until meat is browned. Mix yogurt with water, turmeric, peppers and salt. Pour into the skillet and mix. Bring to a boil, lower heat, cover and cook for 20-25 minutes. Add mushrooms and cook until meat is tender. Uncover and add fried onion slices. Raise heat to evaporate most of the liquid. The only sauce should be what clings to the meat. Serve with poori or chappati, plain rice or pilaf.

Lamb Kofta Surprise

For the Base

1 pound ground lamb
½ medium onion, chopped fine
¼ cup chickpea flour (besan)
1 teaspoon salt
1 teaspoon fresh ginger, grated
2 cloves garlic, chopped
1 serrano pepper
½ teaspoon cayenne pepper
2-3 tablespoons oil

For the Filling

½ cup frozen green peas, thawed
½ teaspoon salt
¼ cup chickpea flour (besan)
3 cloves garlic
1 hot green chili pepper, seeded
½ teaspoon cumin seeds
½ medium onion chopped
Oil for pan frying

Mix base ingredients and set aside. Drain thawed green peas and pat dry with paper towels to remove all moisture. Add filling ingredients into a food processor bowl and pulse a few times. Do not puree. Set aside. Divide meat mixture into 12 portions. Do the same with peas mixture.

Take one portion of meat and roll into a ball, flattening it in your palm. Add a portion of peas and fold over the meat to completely enclose the peas mixture. Repeat the process with all 12 portions. Heat a shallow nonstick pan, add oil and pan fry the meatballs. Remove to a platter. Serve as a snack or in an onion, tomato gravy using 1 recipe of Punjabi masala. Serves 3-4.

Makhani Chicken *(Traditional Butter Chicken)*

2 pounds chicken breast or 3 pounds chicken thighs, boneless

For Marinade

1 cup yogurt
4 tablespoons lemon juice
2 tablespoons vegetable oil
2 teaspoon salt or to taste
1 tablespoon turmeric
1 tablespoon hot red pepper

For Curry

½ cup oil
2 teaspoons cumin seeds
1 inch fresh ginger, finely chopped
1 tablespoon garlic, finely chopped
2 medium yellow onions, sliced
½ cup fresh tomatoes, chopped
2 large hot green peppers
1 tablespoon black pepper
2 teaspoons ground cumin
2 teaspoons coriander powder

Butter masala

1 stick (4 ounces)butter
1 cup onion, sliced
3 green onions, chopped
1 tablespoon paprika
1 teaspoon garam masala

Garnish

¼ cup cilantro
¼ cup sliced red onion
1 medium tomato, sliced
1 tablespoon fresh lemon juice
1 teaspoon paprika
½ teaspoon garam masala

Cut chicken into 2-inch cubes. Mix marinade together and pour over the chicken and refrigerate for 4 hours. Heat oil in a large heavy skillet. Sprinkle cumin seeds, add ginger and garlic and stir for 30 seconds. Remove chicken from marinade and add to the skillet. Cook until brown. Add sliced onions, chopped tomatoes, and green peppers. Cook until tomatoes are soft and chicken is coated. Cook chicken fully on medium heat, turning frequently. Do not add any water. Add leftover marinade, 2-3 tablespoons at a time to prevent sticking. Use all the marinade, continue to cook until chicken is tender and oil separates from the curry. Add red and black pepper, coriander, cumin powder and mix well. Remove chicken from the pan. Add 2 cups of water to the left over curry in the skillet and reduce to half. Pour over chicken.

Melt butter in clean heavy pan. Fry onions until light brown, add green onions and continue to fry until brown. Turn off the heat. Add paprika and garam masala, stir. Add cooked chicken and mix well. Remove to a serving platter. Garnish with cilantro, sliced onions and tomatoes. Sprinkle lemon juice, paprika and garam masala just before serving. Makhani chicken tastes better the day after. So make it a day in advance.

Murg Musallam *(Roasted Chicken)*

For the Rub

1 (2-3 pounds) whole chicken
2-3 teaspoons salt
2 teaspoons paprika
2 teaspoons black pepper
¼ cup plain yogurt
2 tablespoons oil

For Masala

½ cup ghee
3 cups yellow onion, chopped
2 tablespoons fresh ginger, grated
1 tablespoon fresh garlic, chopped
4 tablespoons tomato paste
1 tablespoon cumin powder
2 teaspoons dry methi leaves
1 teaspoon salt, adjust to taste
1 teaspoon paprika
2 teaspoons cayenne pepper
(adjust to taste or omit)
¼ cup whipping cream
2 tablespoons almonds, coarsely crushed
1 teaspoon black poppy seeds
1 tablespoon golden raisins
¼ cup water
½ teaspoon coriander powder
2 pods crushed black cardamom skin
and all

Remove skin from the chicken. Pierce chicken all over with a fork. Rub chicken evenly with a paste of yogurt, salt, paprika and black pepper.

Spread oil over seasoned chicken and in the cavities. Cover and refrigerate overnight. Preheat oven to 400°F and bake chicken on the middle rack for 30 minutes. Lower heat to 350 degrees and bake for ½ hour or until chicken is cooked (leg will move freely from the joint when done).

While the chicken is being baked prepare Masala as below:

Heat ghee to smoking point. Add onions and fry until dark brown. Add ginger, garlic and cook until light brown. Lower heat to medium and add tomato paste. Stir continuously; add ¼ cup water, a little at a time to make a paste. When the oil separates, add the next five spices. Mix quickly and add cream. The mixture will turn milky and light in color. Continue to cook until the oil separates again. Add almonds, poppy seeds and cook for 30 seconds. Add raisins and ¼ cup water. When the mixture bubbles, remove from heat, sprinkle coriander powder and cardamom, cover and let stand for 10 minutes. The masala should be thick but flowing. Place chicken on an ovenproof serving dish and pour all the masala over it. Cover tightly with aluminum foil and bake for 15 minutes at 350°F. Garnish with cilantro, fresh tomatoes and lemon wedges. Carve and serve.

Pork Bhathi *(Pork Loin Roast)*

4 pounds boneless pork loin

Mughlai Marinade

1 cup yellow onion, diced

3 jalapeno peppers or hot green chili peppers

2 inch piece fresh ginger, chopped

2 tablespoons garlic, finely chopped

¼ cup cilantro, chopped

4 teaspoons salt (adjust to taste)

2 teaspoon hot cayenne pepper

1 tablespoon black pepper, crushed

1 teaspoon garlic powder

2 tablespoons lemon juice

¼ cup Worcestershire sauce

2 tablespoons rice vinegar

¼ cup vegetable oil

Coarsely blend onion, green hot pepper, ginger, garlic and cilantro. Add salt, cayenne, black pepper and garlic powder. Make deep slits, about 2 inches apart, on top of the pork loin. Place pork loin in a deep, narrow dish and stuff with the onion mix. Pour lemon juice, Worcestershire sauce and vinegar into the slits. Marinate in the refrigerator for 24 hours, basting 3-4 times with the marinade. Remove from the refrigerator one hour before cooking. Turn oven on at 350°F. Heat oil in a heavy pan or Dutch oven on the stove at high heat. Sear pork loin, fat side down first in the hot oil. Then brown the top and each side. Remove into a baking dish, cover loosely with foil and bake until thermometer inserted in the center reads 155°-160°. It takes about 2 hour per pound of meat to cook well. Cool and slice (diagonal cut). Place in a platter. Pour the juice over the slices. Garnish to serve as desired. Great with pineapple pickle or Kashmiri green apples.

Quick Meat Curry

A frantically busy life has not erased my taste for savory, freshly made food. In fact, just assembling a dish and sitting down to eat it hot from the stove does put one back in touch with the fundamentals of earthly life.

Cooking time: About 1½ hour, including marinating time for meat. There is nothing original about this recipe except the speed with which it is put on the stove to cook. The meat can be of different types, as long as it is more-or-less cubed. Various root vegetables, peeled and cubed can be added 15 minutes before the end of cooking, or when the meat is tender. Green vegetables (beans, spinach), however, should be added 5 to 10 minutes before the end of cooking time.

1 pound meat, cubes/stew size, boneless
Lean pork, or turkey leg meat or chicken

For the Marinade

1 onion
3 cloves garlic, peeled
1 inch segment of fresh ginger, peeled
2 small hot peppers, red or green
1 teaspoon turmeric
2 teaspoon ground cumin
½-1 teaspoon salt
1½ tablespoon oil
3 small potatoes, diced
¾ cup water

Place meat in a mixing bowl. Grind marinade ingredients coarsely in food processor. Add marinade over bowl of meat, mix and leave at room temperature for 20 to 30 minutes (i.e. while you cook the rice, make salad, find chapatis in the freezer, etc.). Heat oil in a decent sized pot (such as a large skillet or Dutch oven or a serious heavy-duty saucepan). Transfer contents of meat bowl into the pot, stirring constantly until spices and meat are browned. The onion component should be nearly transparent by now. Add potatoes and water. Bring to a simmer, lower heat and cook until meat is tender (20 to 30 minutes). If the water seems to be drying up completely, add another ¼ cup once or twice.

Tandoori Chicken

10 pounds chicken leg quarters cleaned and skinned

For Marinade

2 cups plain yogurt
2 medium onions
2 tablespoons vegetable oil
4 tablespoons melted butter
2 tablespoons lemon juice
2 tablespoons wine vinegar
¼ cup tandoori chicken paste
4 teaspoons salt (only if the paste is unsalted)

Garnish & Condiments

½ red onion, sliced
2 tablespoons lemon juice
1 teaspoon cayenne pepper
2 teaspoons salt
2 teaspoons coriander powder
2 teaspoons cayenne pepper (Optional)
6 fresh hot green peppers or
2 tablespoons sliced jalapeno pickles (Optional)
16 lemon wedges
2 tablespoons cilantro chopped

Make deep slits at a slant on chicken legs and thigh meat, about 2 inches apart and place in a bowl or plastic bag. Mix marinade ingredients in a food processor. Pour marinade over the chicken, seal and marinate for at least 4 hours. Mix sliced onions with lemon juice, pepper and salt. Save. Drain chicken out of the marinade and charcoal BBQ on medium heat, turning frequently. When chicken is nearly cooked, baste with the marinade repeatedly. Keep cooked pieces warm in a tightly covered baking dish. Cook remaining marinade in a saucepan until thick and brown. Pour over the cooked chicken and keep covered until ready to serve. Sprinkle lemon juice from the soaked onions over the chicken. Sprinkle coriander powder and cayenne pepper, garnish with sliced onion, hot green pepper, cilantro and lemon wedges. Lemon wedges may be used for added flavor. Serve hot or cold. Serves 12-15.

Several brands of tandoori paste are available in most super markets in the gourmet section or from Indian specialty stores. I prefer Pathak brand

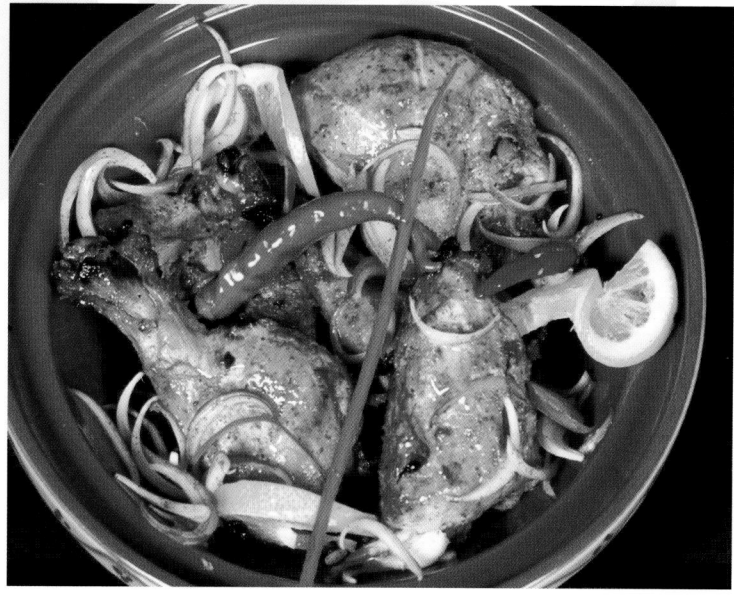

Tandoori Pork Tenderloin

Tandoori is any food cooked in a tandoor (Indian clay oven). When a tandoor is not available, an oven or grill can be used as a substitute. While tandoori chicken is popular throughout the world, tandoori pork is more unusual, yet equally delicious. This simple and straightforward recipe, utilizing easily available ingredients, allows the cook to give an impression of having done much more work!

2 pounds pork tenderloin
2 tablespoons ginger, grated
1 teaspoon granulated garlic or 1 tablespoon fresh minced garlic
1 teaspoon cayenne pepper (or to taste)
1 teaspoon garam masala
1 teaspoon coriander powder
1 teaspoon cumin powder
½ teaspoon turmeric
2 teaspoons salt
2 tablespoons canola oil
2 tablespoons white vinegar

Mix all spices and salt with oil and vinegar. Rub mixture into the pork tenderloin. Marinade in the refrigerator for at least 4 hours, preferably overnight. Bake tenderloin at 350° for one hour or until center is well done (temperature at center should measure 160°). Slice and serve with sliced tomatoes and/or sliced onions that have marinated in lemon juice and salt. This dish can also be used as a filling for tortilla wraps. Serves 4-6.

Crab Curry

2 pounds crabs, (4 medium) cleaned
3 tablespoons oil, divided
1 cup grated coconut
2 small red onions cut into 8 pieces
1 small red onion, finely chopped
1½ tablespoons coriander seeds
8 cloves
1 inch cinnamon stick
3 bay leaves
1¼ teaspoons cumin seeds
¾ teaspoon black cumin seeds
2 dry hot red chilies
6 dry mild red chilies
1 black cardamom
3 small green cardamom
¼ teaspoon mace
6 tablespoons poppy seeds
½ teaspoon ginger paste
½ teaspoon garlic paste
2 tablespoons vinegar
Salt to taste

In a small frying pan heat 1 tablespoon oil and cook quartered onions for 5 minutes. Add coconut and roast until coconut turns pink. Grind to a fine paste and keep aside. Add 1 tablespoon oil to the pan and roast coriander seeds. Add cloves and cinnamon, bay leaves, cumin seeds, cayenne, peppers, black cumin, cardamom, mace and poppy seeds. Roast until spices become aromatic. Grind spices to a fine powder.

Remove the thin crab legs and grind them with a cup of water. Strain the juice and save, or use bottled clam juice. Heat a saucepan, add 1 tablespoon oil and sauté chopped onions. Add ginger and garlic paste and sauté again. Then add the powdered spices and sauté again. Add vinegar, crab or clam juice and the coconut- onion paste. Add crabs and salt to taste and bring to a boil. Do not overcook. Serves 4

Substitute a can of clam juice for juice from ground crab legs.

Crab Masala

8 boiled crabs
1 tablespoon lime juice
1 teaspoon turmeric
1 tablespoon ghee or melted butter
1 tablespoon panch phoran
(five spice mix)
2 bay leaves
¼ cup oil (olive, canola, or mustard)
4 onions, chopped
1 ½ tablespoons cumin powder
2 tablespoons coriander powder
1 teaspoon garam masala
(Mixture of clove, cardamom, cinnamon, mace, red and black pepper)
1 tablespoon ginger root paste
4 cloves garlic paste
Red pepper to taste
1 tablespoon plain yogurt
Large pinch saffron in a cup of warm water
Salt to taste
Chopped cilantro
Whole green chili
Onion and lime cut in rings
Golden raisins, almond, cashew
(optional)

Clean crabs and wash. Marinate in a mix of oil, lemon juice, pinch of turmeric and salt for 10 minutes. In a large saucepan, heat ghee with panch phoran and bay leaves for 10 seconds. Add crabs, brown them, and set aside. In a nonstick pan, heat oil and sauté chopped onion until pink, add cumin and coriander powder, garam masala, ginger, garlic, red pepper and yogurt (15 minutes). Add saffron water and simmer. Add crabs and mix thoroughly, reduce to low heat and simmer for 10 minutes to blend flavors. Adjust salt. Remove from heat and discard bay leaves. Add nuts and raisins. Garnish with cilantro, onion and lime rings. Serve hot with plain basmati rice, fried rice or naan. Serves 6-8 as a main dish. Cooking time 55 minutes.

It is important to wash the crab carefully and check the color of the crab. Crab should be whitish in color. When stirring, take care not to break up the crab.

Fish Curry

2 pounds catfish steaks, 2 inches thick
2 teaspoons salt
2 tablespoons whole-wheat flour
Onion masala
½ cup onion, chopped
1 teaspoon minced ginger
1 tablespoon garlic, chopped
2 teaspoons mustard seeds
1 ½ tablespoons coriander powder
1 teaspoon cayenne pepper
½ teaspoons turmeric
2 teaspoons salt
3 tablespoons olive oil
1 cup chopped tomatoes, fresh or canned
1 cup water
4 tablespoons chopped cilantro, divided
1 teaspoon mango powder (amchur)

Rub fish with salt and whole-wheat flour and let it stand for 2 minutes. Wash fish thoroughly, pat dry, and set aside. Grind onion, ginger, garlic, mustard, coriander, cayenne, turmeric and salt in a blender to a paste. In a large sauté pan heat olive oil over medium heat and sauté the onion masala until it thickens. Add tomatoes and cook for 2 minutes, stirring constantly. Reduce heat, add fish, and cook in the sauce for 5 to 7 minutes. Add water, 2 tablespoons cilantro and mango powder, cover and simmer for 10 minutes or until fish is cooked. Fish will flake easily with a fork. Place in a serving dish and garnish with chopped cilantro. Serves 6.

Macher Jhal *(Bengali Fish Curry)*

This is a popular style of fish curry from Bengal. The fish is first broiled or pan fried and added to a watery but flavorful curry. It can be served as a fish soup, just cut the fish into smaller pieces.

1 pound fish (catfish fillets or any other fish)
1 teaspoon turmeric, divided
1 teaspoon salt, divided
2 tablespoons oil
1 teaspoon nigella seeds
1 hot green chili, chopped
½ teaspoon cayenne pepper
1 teaspoon ginger paste
1 teaspoon garlic paste
3 cups water
Salt to taste
2 tablespoons chopped cilantro leaves

Rub fish with ½ teaspoon salt and ½ teaspoon turmeric. Keep aside for 10 minutes. Rinse and pat dry. Heat broiler and broil fish for 10 minutes on one side, turn over and broil for 4 minutes. Set aside. Heat oil in a saucepan over moderate heat; add nigella and green chili. Mix turmeric, ½ teaspoon salt, cayenne pepper, ginger, garlic paste in a cup of water and pour the mixture into the pan. Add remaining water and bring to a boil. Put the pieces of fish in to the pan and cook for two minutes. Adjust salt. Sprinkle cilantro leaves and serve with steamed rice or roti.

Sour Cream Shrimp or Catfish

1 pound shrimp or cubed catfish
1 cup sour cream
½ teaspoon cayenne pepper
1 teaspoon mustard powder
¼ teaspoon turmeric
¼ teaspoon minced garlic (optional)
2 tablespoons oil
½ teaspoon salt (or as needed)

Mix all ingredients and marinate for 1 to 2 hours. Preheat oven to 350°F. Bake uncovered for 30 to 45 minutes or until the shrimp or fish is tender.

Mustard Fish

4 small whole catfish, cut into 8 pieces
Rub
3 tablespoon lemon juice
¼ teaspoon turmeric
Salt

Spice Paste
¾ tablespoon yogurt
1 ½ tablespoons brown mustard paste
1 tablespoon hot green chili pepper paste
6 tablespoons canola oil
1 teaspoon panch phoran
(cumin, fennel, mustard, nigella, fenugreek seeds)
½ cup water

Garnish
½ cup cilantro, chopped
Lemon slices

Rub catfish pieces with lemon juice, turmeric and salt. Set aside for 15 minutes. Make a paste with yogurt, mustard, green chili paste and 1 teaspoon oil.

In a non-stick fry pan, add 5 tablespoons oil and fry fish for 2 to 3 minutes until fish turns brown in color. Remove from heat and keep warm. Heat 2 teaspoons oil in a pan, add panch phoran and spice paste, fry until aroma is released. Add water and bring to a boil. Simmer for 5 minutes. Add fish and heat for 5 minutes. Remove to serving platter, garnish with lemon slices and chopped cilantro. Serve hot with plain basmati rice. Serves 6. Cooking time 35 minutes.

Parsi Fish *(Fish with Green Coconut Chutney)*

1 pomfret or any other fish, cut in steaks
Salt
Banana leaves
Oil

For Green Chutney
1 cup grated fresh coconut or 1
(6-ounce packet) frozen coconut
2-4 green chilies (Serrano or cayenne)
½ teaspoon cumin seeds
1 cup packed coriander leaves with
tender stems
Few mint leaves
1 teaspoon tamarind pulp or lemon juice
Salt to taste

Clean, wash and dry the fish. Apply a little salt and keep aside for 30 minutes.. Cut each banana leaf into 8x8-inch piece. Take same number of banana leaves as pieces of fish. Heat banana leaves on each side for a few seconds till they are soft. Grind all the ingredients for the chutney to a fine paste. Rinse the fish to remove salt and pat dry. Apply chutney liberally all over the fish. Wrap each piece of fish in a banana leaf, folding sides in and making a packet. Tie firmly with kitchen string. Shallow fry the packets with oil in a frying pan, over low heat, for about 5 minutes. Turn over and cook for 5 minutes on the other side. Cover pan with a lid and cook for another 5 minutes until leaf turns dark and the fish is cooked inside. (This can be tested with a skewer put through the center of the fish. If skewer goes through easily, fish is ready). Serve the fish in its packet. Serve hot.

Frozen banana leaves can be found in Asian stores. Heavy-duty foil may be substituted for the banana leaves and the packets baked at 350ºF for 30 minutes.

Royal Bengal Whole Fish

3 - 4 pounds red fish, snapper or bass or whole tilapia
1 ½ teaspoons salt
1 teaspoon turmeric
½ - 1 cup mustard oil or safflower oil
2 tablespoons fresh ginger, grated
½ cup dry mustard or prepared creole mustard
1 cup fresh tomato, pureed
2 hot green chili peppers, sliced
1 teaspoon nigella seeds
Cilantro leaves to garnish

Have the butcher gut the fish. Make slits 2 inches apart on both sides of the scaled and cleaned fish. Rub salt and turmeric all over. Add a little oil and ginger and let it marinade for at least 3 hours. Mix dry mustard, tomato, chili, and nigella, and rest of the oil into a fine paste. Pour over the fish and secure the baking dish with foil. Bake in oven at 400° F for 20 to 30 minutes. Do not overcook. Uncover and garnish with coriander leaves and serve.

The fish can also be cooked in the microwave – cook for 6 to 8 minutes on high. Check fish for doneness by inserting a toothpick. Serves 6.

In Bengal nigella or kalonji is called black cumin or kalo jeera; not to be mistaken with another spice called kala jeera, shah jeera or black cumin.

1 pound medium or large shrimp, cleaned
2 tablespoon lime juice
1 teaspoon oil

2 tablespoons yogurt
1 teaspoon mustard seed paste
½ small onion, finely chopped
4 cloves garlic, minced
¼ inch fresh ginger, peeled and minced
1 tablespoon hot green chili paste
½ teaspoon turmeric
½ can coconut milk
2 tablespoons oil (canola, olive or mustard)
1 tablespoon panch phoran (five spices)
2 bay leaves
2 tablespoons warm water
Salt to taste (about ¾ teaspoon)
1 teaspoon raisins (optional)
1 tablespoon cilantro, chopped
1 hot green chili pepper to garnish
½ cup green peas (optional)

Peel, de-vein and wash shrimp. Sprinkle with a pinch of salt, lime- juice and oil. Sauté shrimp in a hot non-stick pan & transfer to a plate. Drain water if any.

Blend yogurt, mustard, onion, garlic, ginger, green chili and turmeric with coconut milk. In a non-stick pan, heat oil with five spices and bay leaves for about 15 seconds. When the aroma arises, add yogurt mixture. Stir for 10 minutes, add water to mixture and cook until it begins to boil. Add shrimp and simmer for 10 minutes on low heat. Add raisins and salt. When oil comes to the top, remove from heat and discard bay leaves. Transfer the shrimp curry to a serving bowl. Garnish with chopped cilantro and whole hot green chili peppers.

Serve with plain basmati rice or naan. Serves 4 as a main dish. Cooking time 30 minutes.

Rubbing your hands with lemon juice and salt after using any seafood removes odors.

Shrimp in Yogurt Sauce

1½ pounds large shrimp (shelled and cleaned)
4 tablespoons clarified butter (ghee)
2 medium onions, thinly sliced
8 cloves garlic, chopped
1 teaspoon cayenne pepper
1 tablespoon ginger paste
8 ounces plain yogurt
2 green cardamoms
4 cloves
2-inch stick cinnamon
2 bay leaves
1 teaspoon sugar
Salt to taste, about 1 teaspoon

Mix all the ingredients except shrimp and butter. Heat butter in a microwave safe 8x 8x2 inch-baking dish for about 2 minutes on high heat.

Crush cardamom, cloves, cinnamon and bay leaves together. Except for shrimp add all ingredients to the dish. Cook on low heat for 10 minutes. Remove the dish, add shrimp and mix well. Cover with a piece of wax paper and cook on low heat for 5-7 minutes. Serve with cooked piping hot rice. Serves 6.

Variation: Sauté onions in a small amount of oil prior to adding to the shrimp. It imparts a caramel taste to the preparation.

Microwave ovens vary considerably in their power. While cooking shrimp or other seafood in the microwave, it is better to err on the side of cooking it for a shorter duration and rechecking the dish. Overcooking will toughen the seafood.

Shrimp and Eggplant Curry

1 pound medium shrimp
1 large eggplant
1 lemon size ball tamarind, soaked in ½ cup water
½ medium onion
6-8 cloves garlic
4 dry hot red chilies
1½ tablespoons coriander seeds
3 tablespoons oil
1 large onion, chopped fine
10-12 ounces coconut milk
1½ teaspoons salt

Shell, de-vein, wash and drain the shrimp. Wash and trim the eggplant. Cut into 1½-inch cubes (do not peel). Deep fry on moderately high heat for a few minutes till cooked. Drain on paper towels. Prepare tamarind pulp by mashing tamarind in the and straining the pulp. Grind onion, garlic, red chilies and coriander seeds to a paste in a blender .Add a small amount of tamarind pulp to the paste. Heat 3 tablespoons vegetable oil in a saucepan over moderate heat. Sauté chopped onion till pink, not brown. Add shrimp sauté for 2 minutes. Add ground onion paste and sauté till a thin film of oil appears on the surface. Add fried eggplant, coconut milk and adjust salt to taste. Simmer for 2-3 minutes. Serve with rice. Serves 6.

Steamed Shrimp

1 pound shrimp, peeled and cleaned
½ cup very finely chopped onion
¼ cup very finely chopped tomatoes
¼ cup very finely chopped cilantro
5-7 serrano peppers, kept whole
2 tablespoons mustard oil
½ teaspoon ground mustard seeds
½ teaspoon salt or to taste
½ teaspoon turmeric

De-vein, wash and drain the shrimp. Mix all ingredients together and steam in a steamer for 20 to 25 minutes. Serves 4.

Mustard oil is available in Indian grocery stores.

Very Easy Fish Curry

4 tilapia fish filets (frozen or fresh), about 1 pound
2 tablespoons canola oil
1 small onion, chopped (about ¾ cup)
1 (14 ounce) can coconut milk
½ teaspoon garlic powder, or 1 teaspoon fresh minced garlic
2 teaspoons peeled and chopped or finely shredded fresh ginger
1 ½ teaspoons coriander powder
½-1 teaspoon cayenne pepper, to taste
½-1 teaspoon tamarind pulp (available at Oriental stores)
1 teaspoon salt, or to taste
1 hot green chili pepper, slit in half

Rub ½ teaspoon salt on the fish and marinate for 15 minutes. Heat oil in a 10-inch sauté pan. Sauté chopped onions over moderate heat until pink for about 3-4 minutes. Add coconut milk, garlic, ginger, cayenne pepper coriander powder and salt to taste. Add tilapia fillets and bring to a boil. Put the slit green chili on top. Simmer for 5 minutes or until fish is firm. Serve with plain basmati rice.

Serves 2-4.

Fusion Foods

When we settled on the shores of our adopted land, a transformation started in all aspects of our lives. Cuisine was no exception and our culinary horizons began to expand. Not only did we become aware of different cooking techniques, we also started using ingredients in different ways. As we became more absorbed into the society, we incorporated the best of Louisiana into our traditions.

Louisiana, like India, is known the world over for its cuisine, culture and hospitality. Though heavily influenced by French and Creole cuisine, Louisiana uses rice and seafood in its fare. Many parallels in Indian and Louisiana cuisine can be found. What rice biryani is to India, jambalaya is to Louisiana. In India, red beans and rice are seasoned with tomatoes and spices. In Louisiana sausage is used. The Indian Alu-Bondas become shrimp and boudin balls in South Louisiana. Palak-Paneer and Spinach Madeline differ only in the type of spices and cheese used. Similarly, okra and eggplant find a culinary encore in both cultures. Use of the trinity (onion, celery and bell-pepper) along with garlic in Louisiana cuisine can be compared with the use of onion, tomato, ginger and garlic in most North Indian cooking. Liberal use of pepper, too, is common. Many Indian recipes are adapted to use Tabasco Pepper sauce from Louisiana's Avery Island.

America is a melting pot of the world where all cultures survive with equal enthusiasm. Exposure to other cuisines such as Chinese, Italian, Mexican, Greek, Armenian has also influenced the Indian recipes in this section. Use of cilantro, popularized by Mexican cuisine is used extensively in Indian recipes.

Banaras Italian Eggplant

That's right, you read right. Both Varanasi (formerly Banaras) region of Uttar Pradesh and Southern Italy abound in wonderful varieties of eggplant. I learnt a recipe featuring lots of garlic, olive oil, balsamic vinegar and basil from a Sicilian American living in Washington, D. C. For a whole year during graduation, In Varanasi I made do with what I found there. Both versions have been a complete hit, even among the rare people (at my table, anyway) who say they "don't like eggplant."

1 large eggplant, about 2 pounds
Salt
5 cloves garlic, sliced
Juice of one lime
1/3 cup chopped cilantro leaves
4-5 tablespoons peanut or vegetable oil for frying

Cube or thinly slice eggplant. Place in colander, salt thoroughly (about 1 ½ tablespoons) and mix. Put plate under colander and let the liquid drain out for at least 20 minutes, but you could let it sit all day if you've got to go somewhere.

Heat 3 tablespoons oil in a *karhai*, heavy skillet or wok. Fry garlic slices over medium heat for what feels like a long time, actually about five minutes—until they are very brown. Add the drained eggplant and cook to death, stirring frequently. If they stick to the pan too much, add more oil, a bit at a time. The eggplant should almost be like a dry dip or spread when you finish, but with some of the pieces and shapes still discernible. Take off the heat and spoon into a sturdy (pottery or glass) serving bowl. Squeeze the limejuice on the eggplant, sprinkle about 1/3 cup cleaned and chopped cilantro leaves and then minimally toss everything together. Serve as a side dish or as an appetizer with crackers or fancy bread.

Carrot Cake

For cake
2 cups all purpose flour
2 cups sugar
3 teaspoons cinnamon
2 teaspoons baking soda
1 teaspoon salt
1½ cups oil
4 eggs
3 cups carrots, grated (6-7 medium carrots)

For Icing
1 stick butter
1 (8-ounce) package cream cheese
1 (16-ounce) box powdered sugar
2 teaspoons vanilla
Chopped pecans (optional)

Mix all the dry ingredients. Add all other ingredients and mix at medium speed for 2 minutes.

Grease and flour two or three 9 inch round cake pans. Pour batter equally in all the pans. Bake in a pre-heated oven at 350°F for 30 to 35 minutes. Cool in pans for 5 minutes. Remove from pans and cool completely on racks.

Icing: Cream butter and cream cheese, add vanilla and mix, add sugar. Mix well until creamy. Add pecans and mix. Apply icing when cakes have cooled. Spread between cake layers, on sides and top of cake. Serves 12.

Chicken and Sausage Gumbo *By Chef John Folse*

Preparation Time: 2 Hours

Yields: 8–10 Servings

Comment:

Chicken and sausage are the most popular gumbo ingredients in Louisiana. The ingredients were readily available since most Cajun families raised chickens and made a variety of sausages. Oysters were often added to this everyday dish for a special Sunday or holiday version.

1 (5-pound) stewing hen
1 pound smoked sausage or andouille
1 cup oil
1½ cups flour
2 cups diced onions
2 cups diced celery
1 cup diced bell peppers
¼ cup minced garlic
3 quarts chicken stock
24 button mushrooms
2 cups sliced green onions
1 bay leaf
sprig of thyme
1 tbsp chopped basil
salt and cracked black pepper to taste
Louisiana hot sauce to taste
½ cup chopped parsley
cooked white rice

Using a sharp boning knife, cut hen into 8–10 serving pieces. Remove as much fat as possible. Cut smoked sausage or andouille into ½-inch slices and set aside. In a 2-gallon stockpot, heat oil over medium-high heat. Whisk in flour, stirring constantly until golden brown roux is achieved. Stir in onions, celery, bell peppers and garlic. Sauté 3–5 minutes or until vegetables are wilted. Blend chicken and sausage into vegetable mixture, and sauté approximately 15 minutes. Add chicken stock, one ladle at a time, stirring constantly. Bring to a rolling boil, reduce to simmer and cook approximately 1 hour. Skim any fat or oil that rises to top of pot. Stir in mushrooms, green onions, bay leaf, thyme and basil. Season to taste using salt, pepper and hot sauce. Cook an additional 1–2 hours, if necessary, until chicken is tender and falling apart. Stir in parsley and adjust seasonings. Serve over hot white rice.

You may wish to boil chicken 1–2 hours before beginning gumbo. Reserve stock, bone chicken and use meat and stock in gumbo.

Chicken and Sausage Jambalaya *By Chef John Folse*

Preparation Time: 2 Hours

Yields: 15–20 Servings

Comment:

In the early 1700s, Spanish settlers in New Orleans brought their famous paella. Since the traditional Spanish ingredients for paella were not found in South Louisiana, the recipe was adapted to indigenous ingredients. Oysters and crawfish replaced clams and mussels, and fresh pork or andouille took the place of cured ham. The new dish was influenced by many different cultures, including the Africans who contributed their rice or *yaya* to jambalaya. The French later named the dish *Jambon a la yaya*, meaning ham with rice.

3 pounds chicken, cut into 2-inch pieces
2 pounds sliced smoked sausage
¼ cup shortening or bacon drippings
2 cups diced onions
2 cups diced celery
1 cup diced bell peppers
½ cup minced garlic
8 cups beef or chicken stock
2 cups sliced mushrooms
1 cup sliced green onions
½ cup chopped parsley
salt and cayenne pepper to taste
Louisiana hot sauce to taste
5 cups uncooked long-grain rice

In a 7-quart cast iron Dutch oven, heat shortening or bacon drippings over medium-high heat. Sauté chicken 30 minutes or until dark brown on all sides and beginning to stick to bottom of pot. This process is important because jambalaya's brown color is derived from the color of the meat. Add smoked sausage and stir fry 10–15 minutes. Tilt pot to one side and ladle out all oil, except 1 large cooking spoonful. Add onions, celery, bell peppers and garlic. Continue cooking until all vegetables are well caramelized, being careful not to scorch them. Pour in stock, bring to a rolling boil then reduce heat to simmer. Cook 15 minutes to allow flavors to develop. Stir in mushrooms, green onions and parsley. Season with salt, cayenne pepper and hot sauce. If desired, slightly over-season dish since rice has not yet been added. Add rice, reduce heat to low, cover and cook 30–45 minutes. Stir every 15 minutes. Do not uncover except to stir.

Chutney Appetizer

This dish was inspired by the popular pepper jelly and cream cheese appetizer in Louisiana and became an instant favorite. Feel free to experiment with your favorite chutney or pickle.

1 (8-ounce) packet cream cheese
½ cup Chunda (a sweet and sour mango pickle) or Major Grey's mango chutney.
Toast points or assorted crackers of your choice

Put the cream cheese on a serving plate. Warm the Chunda pickle in the microwave to soften and pour over the cream cheese. Serve at room temperature with toast points or assorted crackers.

Chunda pickle is available at Indian grocery stores. Laxmi brand is preferred.

Cilantro Vinaigrette

This is a fresh dressing that is easy to make and adds a unique taste to your salad.

½ cup chopped cilantro
Juice of ½ a lemon
1 teaspoon sugar or 1 packet artificial sweetener
½ teaspoon salt
Freshly ground black pepper, to taste
¼ cup extra virgin olive oil

Mix cilantro, lemon juice, sugar or artificial sweetener, salt and black pepper in a glass bowl. Using a whisk, add olive oil in a steady stream and whisk until all the oil is incorporated in the dressing. Adjust salt and pepper to taste. Serve over salad greens or with chicken tikka. Makes ½ cup dressing.

1 package (8-ounce) Aunt Jemima's Easy Corn Bread mix
2 teaspoons dry kasoori methi or 2 tablespoon fresh methi

¼ teaspoon ajwain
¼ teaspoon black pepper
¼ teaspoon cayenne pepper (add more or less to taste)
¼ teaspoon salt
1 tablespoon hot green pepper, finely chopped
1 tablespoon fresh ginger, grated
2 tablespoons fresh ginger, chopped
2 tablespoons melted butter
2 eggs
1 cup milk
3 tablespoons oil, divided

In a bowl whisk together the first 6 (dry) ingredients. Add the next 3 (fresh) ingredients and mix well. Add butter and 1 tablespoon oil; swirl together to disperse evenly. Lightly beat egg and mix with milk. Pour liquid into the flour mix and mix with a whisk until the batter is smooth & without lumps! Preheat oven to 375°F. Heat remaining 2 tablespoons oil in an ovenproof heavy skillet (use cast iron for best result) and heat until hot and slightly smoky. Quickly pour the batter into the hot oil, spread evenly and bake for 18 to 20 min. Check for doneness with a toothpick or a metal tester. Serve hot! Serves 6-8.

Death By Chocolate (Kathleen Babineaux Blanco Governor of Louisiana)

2 boxes of Devil's Food Cake Mix (baked as directed)
½ cup Kaluha
3 large boxes of chocolate Jell-O mix
3 large containers of Cool Whip Lite
2 Bags of Heath Bar crumbles

Step 1

Cake- Bake two cakes as directed on the box.

Step 2

Upon taking the cake out of the oven, break it up or poke holes in it and pour ¼ cup of Kaluha over the cake.

Place a layer of broken cake pieces at the bottom of your serving dish. (The dish should be about 6-8 inches deep and for cosmetic purposes it should be clear.)

Step 3

Jell-O Silk Pie Mix- Mix according to directions on the box with fat free milk.

Apply half of the mixture to form a layer of "silk" over the cake pieces.

Step 4

Cool Whip- Apply half to the Cool Whip to form a layer over the Silk Pie Mix.

Step 5

Sprinkle one bag of Heath Bar Crumbles over the cool whip layer.

Step 6

Add second cake to top if Heath layer. Repeat Steps 2-5.

Place covered in a refrigerator until ready to serve.

Eggplant and Spinach Parmesan

1 large eggplant
1 cup bread crumbs
2 tablespoons butter
1 ½ tablespoons all- purpose flour
1 ½ cups non-fat milk
 Pinch each of salt, basil, garlic powder
oregano and sugar
1 (10 ounce) package frozen spinach
2 tablespoons olive oil
¼ teaspoon salt
1 (26 ounce) bottle Ragu tomato sauce
1 package (8-ounce) shredded
Mozzarella cheese
½ cup Parmesan cheese

Eggplant

Preheat oven to 450°F. Peel the eggplant and make thick slices lengthwise. Soak pieces in water for about 5 minutes. Remove and drain well. Roll each piece in breadcrumbs. Arrange pieces on a large greased cookie sheet. Cover cookie sheet with aluminum foil. Place in preheated oven and cook until eggplant is just tender.

White Sauce

In large saucepan melt butter and add flour. Cook for 2 minutes without browning. Slowly add milk and stir the mixture until well blended. Add a pinch each of salt, basil, garlic powder, oregano and sugar. Cook until the mixture thickenes.

Spinach-White Sauce

Thaw spinach in a large microwave safe-bowl and add 2 tablespoons olive oil, ½ tsp salt, and a pinch each of basil, garlic powder, oregano and sugar. Mix all ingredients and cook the mixture in a microwave for 3 minutes. Add cooked spinach mixture to the prepared white sauce and mix well.

Baking Process

In a large greased baking pan spread Ragu sauce evenly at the bottom. Arrange baked eggplant side-by-side on top of the sauce. Sprinkle half of mozzarella cheese on top of eggplant. Spread spinach-white sauce on top of cheese. Spread remaining Ragu sauce on top of spinach -white sauce.

Sprinkle remaining mozzarella. Top the layer with Parmesan cheese. Bake in preheated oven for 15 minutes until cheese has melted and the sauce starts to bubble. Cut into 12 individual pieces. Serve with toasted Italian bread or over pasta.

Louisiana Seafood Gumbo *By Chef John Folse*

Prep Time: 1 Hour

Yields: 12 Servings

Comment:

Seafood gumbo is the premier soup of Cajun Country, and it is known worldwide as the dish to seek out when visiting South Louisiana. Every Louisiana home has its own unique ingredients and methods for cooking gumbo.

1 pound (35-count) shrimp, peeled and de-veined
1 pound jumbo lump crabmeat
2 dozen shucked oysters, reserve liquid
1 pound claw crabmeat
3 quarts shellfish stock
1 cup vegetable oil
1 cup flour
2 cups onions, diced
1 cup celery, diced
1 cup bell peppers, diced
¼ cup garlic, minced
½ pound Andouille sausage, sliced
1 cup frozen okra, chopped
2 cups green onions, sliced
½ cup parsley, chopped
salt and cayenne pepper to taste
Louisiana hot sauce to taste

In a 7-quart cast iron Dutch oven, heat oil over medium-high heat. Whisk in flour, stirring constantly until brown roux is achieved. (See roux recipes.) Add onions, celery, bell peppers and garlic. Sauté for 3–5 minutes or until vegetables are wilted. Blend in andouille sausage and sauté an additional 3–5 minutes. Stir in claw crabmeat, ½ cup shrimp and okra. Slowly add hot shellfish stock, one ladle at a time, stirring constantly. Bring to a low boil, reduce to simmer and cook for 30 minutes. If necessary, additional stock may be used to retain volume. Add green onions and parsley. Season to taste using salt, cayenne and hot sauce. Fold in shrimp, lump crabmeat, oysters and reserved oyster liquid. Return to a low boil and cook for approximately 5 minutes. Adjust seasonings if necessary. Serve over cooked rice.

Mixed Fruit Sasum *(Fruit Salad with Coconut-Mustard Dressing)*

1 apple, cubed (1 cup)
1 orange, peeled, sectioned (1 cup)
1 banana, peeled, cut lengthwise and sliced
1 ripe mango chopped
1 (8-ounce) can pineapple chunks
1 teaspoon tamarind pulp or pulp made from 3- inch piece of tamarind
½ cup mango pulp
2 teaspoons mustard, ground
1 teaspoon cayenne pepper
1 teaspoon salt
2 tablespoons brown sugar
½ to ¾ can (14-ounce) coconut milk

Drain and save juice from pineapple. Mix all fruits in a large bowl. Mix mango pulp with ¼ cup of pineapple juice. Add to the fruits. Add remaining ingredients and mix well. Chill prior to serving. Serves 8.

One can use a single or a combination of fruits such as grapes, bananas, pineapple, peaches, nectarines etc. The overall flavor is sweet and sour and spicy. Decrease the amount of mango pulp and brown sugar and use the dressing over boiled shrimp in place of remoulade dressing.

Mixed Vegetable Pie

16-ounce package of mixed vegetables
1 potato, diced
2 tomatoes
½ teaspoon ginger-garlic paste
2 medium onions, chopped
Cayenne powder
Coriander powder
Salt to taste
2 piecrust shells

In a pot, add 2 tablespoons of oil and cook the vegetables and potato. Add tomatoes, garlic, ginger paste, spices and salt. Cook vegetables for 8-10 minutes on medium heat then simmer for 5 minutes on low heat. In an 8- inch round baking dish, place the pie shell. Spread evenly the cooked vegetable mixture. Place another pie shell covering the vegetable mixture and press the edges. Make slight cuts with a pizza cutter so that when baked, you can easily get 8 pie pieces. Bake at 350° F, for about 30 minutes or until crust is golden brown. Cut the pie with a pizza cutter and serve with cilantro chutney or ketchup.

Jambalaya

This recipe has been shared by a four-time company-wide United Way Jambalaya Cook-Off winner. This is also a fund-raiser recipe for Sharing Shores.

17 large onions, chopped
3 stems of celery, chopped
12 green or red bell peppers, chopped
30 garlic cloves, minced
16 pounds spicy garlic sausage, cut into thin rounds
14 pounds chicken breast, cut into small pieces
12 pounds parboiled white rice
10 chicken bullions
1 bottle-1 Step Chicken Jambalaya Seasoning
1 bottle kitchen bouquet
6 tablespoons Tony's seasoning
5 tablespoons white/black pepper
8 tablespoons ground cayenne pepper
7 teaspoons dried thyme
2 teaspoons oregano
2 bunches parsley, chopped
8 bunches shallots, chopped
3 gallons and 4 cups water
2 cups oil
Salt, to taste

Heat 1 cup oil in a jambalaya pot. Add sausages, 5 cloves of minced garlic, 2 tablespoon Tony's seasoning and cook until all water has evaporated and sausages turn brown. Remove.

Add chicken pieces, 5 cloves of minced garlic, 2 tablespoon Tony's seasoning and salt. Cook until chicken turns white and almost 70% done (pink center). Remove.

Drain all fat from the pot. Add 1-cup oil and add onion, celery, bell pepper, remainder of minced garlic, 2 tablespoon Tony's seasoning and salt. Cook until vegetables are tender and remaining water has evaporated.

Add cooked sausage and chicken. Mix well and cook for 5 more minutes. Add remaining water and all other ingredients except rice, shallots and parsley. Turn heat on high until water comes to a boil. Season with salt to taste. Add rice and keep stirring until water comes to boil again. Turn the heat to very low, cover the pot and leave it undisturbed for 20 minutes.

Open the lid and add cilantro/parsley. Mix well, cover again and turn off the heat. Let it rest until all the water is absorbed. Serve hot with salad, rolls and beans. Serves 100.

Moong Bean Soup

1 cup whole moong beans, washed and soaked for 2 hours
5 cups water and ham bone or chicken stock or water alone
1 teaspoon turmeric
1 teaspoon salt
½ teaspoon red pepper
2 tablespoon butter
1 medium onion sliced
1 teaspoon cumin seeds, roasted and ground
1 tablespoon fresh ginger, grated
Juice of a lemon
Crème Fraîche

Heat a 3-quart saucepan. Add water and ham bone or chicken stock and bring to boil. Drain the beans and add to the boiling water. Add salt, pepper, and turmeric. Cook until beans are soft (45minutes). Discard bone. Puree half of the soup in a blender. Return to the pan. In a sauté pan, sauté onions in butter until brown, about 7 minutes. Add cumin and ginger. Mix and add to the soup. Cook for 10 minutes on low heat. Add juice of one lemon. Adjust salt and pepper to taste. Serve hot in soup bowls, topped with a teaspoon of Crème Fraîche. Serves 8.

Quick Jambalaya

1 cup rice
5-6 green onions
½ medium onion
1 pound sausage sliced in ½-inch pieces
1 teaspoon dried parsley flakes
½ cup celery, chopped
1 can beef or chicken broth
½ cup water
1-2 teaspoons Lee & Perrins Worcestershire sauce
½ teaspoon black pepper
½ teaspoon cayenne pepper, optional
1 teaspoon salt

Mix all ingredients in an ovenproof casserole dish. Bake uncovered at 350°F for 45 minutes. Mix well and let stand for 5 to 10 minutes. Serve hot.

Variation

Use one 8-ounce can of tomato sauce instead of water. Recipe can be doubled. Bake at 375°F for 40-45 minutes.

Savory Potato - Scallion Chowder

2 pounds potatoes (approx. 3-4 large or 6-10 small)
1 bunch of scallions
2 tablespoons vegetable oil or butter
1 teaspoon dried marjoram or oregano
1 quart milk
2 ½ teaspoons salt, to taste
Freshly ground black pepper (red pepper flakes may be preferred by some)

Wash and boil the potatoes (cutting larger ones in half). Rinse in cold water and peel. Mash coarsely with your hands. Clean (trim off any root hairs and wilted green ends) and chop scallions, both green and white parts. Lightly fry the scallions in the vegetable oil or butter in a large saucepan. Sprinkle the herbs over the onions and stir for a few seconds. Lower the heat drastically; add a spoonful of mashed potatoes to the mixture in the pan. Stir, adding about a third of a cup of milk. Stirr continuously until you get a soupy porridge consistency. Note that the potato does not have to be mixed perfectly, as we are aiming for a lumpy, rather than smooth soup. Mix in the rest of the potatoes. Add the rest of the milk, mixing as you go, and simmer until warmed through. Add water, ¼ cup at a time, if necessary. Add salt and pepper to taste. Serve hot.

Shrimp in Mango - Coconut Sauce

1 pound shrimp, boiled, peeled and deveined
½ pound lump crab meat (optional)
1 tablespoon butter
½ teaspoon olive oil
2 shallots or ½ onion, chopped fine
½ teaspoon turmeric
1 can coconut milk
2 tablespoons mango puree
Salt and pepper to taste
1 teaspoon garam masala
2 tablespoons chopped cilantro

Heat oil and butter in a sauté pan, add shallots and sauté over medium heat for 5 minutes. Do not brown the shallots. Add turmeric, coconut milk and mango puree. Reduce sauce by 1/3. Add shrimp, salt and pepper and mix well. Gently fold in the crabmeat and heat until warm. Top with garam masala and cilantro. Serve with jasmine or basmati rice, flavored with coconut flakes. Serves 8. Cooking time 20 minutes

Variation

1 tsp of mustard seeds and ½ tsp of chopped ginger can be used to add flavor. Add mustard seeds in hot oil before the onions. Mango can be omitted.

Shrimp Balls with Dipping Sauce

2 pounds Yukon Gold potatoes
1 pound medium Louisiana shrimp, boiled and peeled
1 small onion, chopped fine
1 bunch green onions, chopped fine including tops
½ cup fresh cilantro, chopped
2 Serrano chilies, seeded and chopped fine
2 tablespoons fresh ginger, chopped or grated
1 tablespoon coriander seeds
1 teaspoon turmeric powder
1½ teaspoon salt
2 eggs for egg-wash
2 cups seasoned breadcrumbs
Oil for frying
Tiger Sauce

Boil potatoes. Peel and mash with a fork in a large bowl. In a food processor, process the shrimp to a rough chop. Add shrimp and next 8 ingredients to the potatoes. Mix with hand until all ingredients are well incorporated. In the palm of your hand, make 1 ½ - inch round balls. Place on a cookie sheet and chill for 1 to 2 hours. Heat the oil in a deep fryer or a frying pan to 350°F. Dip the balls in egg wash and roll in the breadcrumbs. Place the balls in hot oil in small batches. The balls will float to the top when done. They will be golden brown in appearance. Do not overcook. Keep them warm in the oven while you fry the remaining balls. Serve with Tiger sauce as an appetizer. Makes 50 balls. Serves a party of 10-12 people.

If preparing the balls ahead of time, dip in egg-wash and breadcrumbs only just before frying.

Spicy Potato Muffins

For the Batter

1 cup Cream of Wheat or sooji
3 tablespoons oil
2 cups plain yogurt
½ cup water
½ teaspoon salt
1 ½ teaspoons baking powder
¼ cup rice flour
¼ cup cornmeal
½ teaspoon cumin seeds
2 hot green peppers, chopped fine
4 teaspoons chopped fresh cilantro

For the Filling

3 medium potatoes, medium dice
2 tablespoons oil
½ teaspoon cumin seeds
½ teaspoon coriander powder
1 teaspoon cayenne pepper
¼ teaspoon garam masala
1 teaspoon salt
1 teaspoon mango powder (amchur)

Preheat oven to 350ºF. Mix ingredients for the batter and set aside for 15 minutes. For the filling, heat oil in a sauté pan and roast cumin seeds, add potatoes, cumin, coriander, cayenne, garam masala and salt and stir-fry. Spray a muffin pan with nonstick spray. Fill cup up to $1/3$ with batter, add a layer of potato filling (1 tablespoon), then another layer of batter. Bake at 350ºF for 25 minutes. Makes 12 large or 24 small muffins.

Breads, Parathas Pooris and Rice

Bread

Unlike the western diet, the eastern diet does not feature meat as the main course. Bread and/or rice are the main attraction while vegetables and meat, are the 'sides'. Even among the eastern countries, India, developed a cuisine that is predominantly vegetarian. Waves of invaders influenced India's cuisine, which can be seen in the leavened breads of the Middle East; naans and kulchas to the regular bread of the British.

Being a vegetarian or a non-vegetarian is influenced mainly by religious, geographical or financial reasons; but everyone eats bread or rice. Wheat is grown in North India and whole-wheat flour is used to make bread and some form of bread is eaten at all meals with rice is served for Sunday lunch. In the central and eastern regions where rice is also grown, bread is served at all meals, with rice being served at lunch. In the southern regions where rice is grown in abundance, rice in some form or the other is served at all meals, while bread is seldom served.

Breads can be divided into three categories, rotis, parathas and pooris. They are made with whole-wheat flour and are unleavened. Rotis are the everyday bread. Flour is mixed with water to form dough, rolled out and cooked lightly on both sides and then cooked until done on direct heat. Chapati and phulka are similar and addition of other flours and spices adds variety. Others are tandoori roti (baked in a tandoor) and rumali roti (wafer thin bread).

Parathas are sprinkled with oil or ghee and dusted with dry flour halfway through rolling. The flattened disc is then folded a couple of times and then rolled out again. This gives flakiness to the paratha. It is cooked completely on the griddle; oil is applied liberally to both sides and cooked until crisp. Parathas can be stuffed with potatoes, peas, radishes, cauliflower and even dals. Spices and herbs can be added to the paratha.

Pooris are more for festive occasions. Pooris are made at large gatherings, as frying is quicker than cooking parathas. Like parathas, pooris can be stuffed with potatoes, peas and dals. Luchies are simply pooris made with all-purpose flour.

Leavened breads are made with all-purpose flour. Yogurt, milk, or butter is used to make dough and the dough is left to rise overnight. Naans and kulcha are cooked, traditionally, in a tandoor, whereas Bhatura are fried. Naans and kulcha can be stuffed with onions, potatoes, mint and spices. From the poorest to the richest, from the simplest roti to the most exotic naan, bread in some form or other is an integral part of the Indian meal.

Bhakri *(Gujarati Naan)*

1 cup whole wheat flour
½ teaspoon salt
2 tablespoon oil
½ cup water
Stick butter or margarine

Mix flour and salt. Spread oil evenly on flour/salt mix and blend well by hand. Bind the flour mix by slowly adding water. Knead the dough for about one minute or till soft and smooth. Cut the dough into eight equal portions. Roll out each portion into a 5-inch disc. Heat skillet on medium heat and cook each side of the bhakri for about one minute. Take it off the skillet and cook each side directly on the *gas* burner till brown spots are visible. Apply butter sparingly over one side of the cooked bhakri.

Roti

1 cup aata (wheat chapati flour)
½ teaspoon salt (optional)
½ cup water plus 2 tablespoons if needed

Mix aata, salt and water and make dough. Knead for a few minutes till dough is soft and pliant. Divide dough into balls. Place some dry aata in an 8-inch plate. Sprinkle a ball with the dry aata and roll out into a 6-inch disc. Heat a griddle to medium-high heat. On another burner, place a cake cooling rack and heat burner on high. Place the roti on the griddle and let it cook. When soft brown spots appear on the underside of the roti, flip it over.

Cook second side similarly. Pick roti up with tongs and place the first side on the cake rack. Within a few seconds, the roti will puff up. Flip it over and take off the heat after a few seconds. Alternatively, continue to cook on the griddle and use a kitchen towel or folded paper towel to press the roti all around, allowing it to puff up. Spread butter on one side and serve. Makes 6 rotis.

Palak Roti *(Spinach Roti)*

1 cup aata (wheat chapati flour)
½ cup frozen spinach, thawed
1/8 to ¼ cup water
½ teaspoon salt
¼ teaspoon cumin seeds

Puree spinach with water. Mix aata with salt and cumin. Make dough with spinach puree.

Divide dough in 6 pieces. Roll each piece and make roti or paratha. Makes 6 rotis.

Tomato Roti

1 cup aata (wheat chapati flour)
½ cup tomato sauce
¼ teaspoon cayenne pepper

Make dough with the above ingredients, like plain roti and proceed similarly. Makes 6 rotis.

Tandoori Roti

1 cup aata (wheat chapati flour)
1 tablespoon butter
½ teaspoon salt
¼ teaspoon ajwain
½ cup buttermilk

Make dough. Follow directions for roti. Cook on one side on a heated griddle. Heat oven to broil with the rack on the highest shelf. Place 6 rotis on a cookie sheet, uncooked side up. Slide tray under the broiler and broil till roti puffs up and brown spots appear. Butter and serve hot. Makes 6 rotis.

Makki Ki Roti *(Punjabi Corn Bread)*

3 cups makki ka atta (fine ground corn meal)

2 teaspoons salt, adjust to taste

¼ teaspoon baking powder

2 tablespoons melted butter

1¼ cups boiling water (may add up to ¼ cup more if the meal is too coarse)

Mix cornmeal, salt and baking soda in a bowl. Add butter and rub together to mix well. Make a well in the center of the flour and pour boiling water in the well. Mix using a wooden spatula and press the mixture in a mound to the side of the bowl. Take ¼ portion of the mixture and knead with the heel of the hand to make pliable dough. Wet your hand with warm water and knead until the dough is soft. Make two balls, flatten one ball between the palms of hands. Place on a dampened cheesecloth and pat into a circular disc about 1/8 inch thick and 4-5 inches in diameter. Place a heavy skillet on medium- high burner, oil lightly with a brush and gently place the roti on the skillet starting from one edge and laying it flat. If a bubble forms in the middle, perforate with a knife to release the air. Cook on one side for about one minute, turn over and cook the other side for one minute. Lightly butter the surface and turn roti over again. Adjust the time to make sure that the bread is cooked on both sides. Butter liberally and serve hot. The bread will become hard and crumbly when cold. Serve with sarson ka saag. Makes 8-10 rotis.

Paratha

2 cup aata (wheat chapati flour)
Pinch of salt
¾ to 1cup water
Additional flour for rolling
Oil or butter for pan-frying

Mix aata, salt and water and make dough. Knead till dough is soft and pliant. Coat the dough evenly with a few drops of oil and divide into ten-twelve balls. Heat a griddle to medium high. (*Proper temperature is critical! Too hot will burn the prathas and if not heated enough the prathas will dry and toughen*). Dust rolling surface with dry flour and roll out the balls into a 6-inch discs. Sprinkle a few drops of oil on the disc and spread it evenly with a pastry brush or the back of a spoon. Fold the disc in half and then again in half, forming a triangle. Now roll again into a 6 to 7-inch triangle. Place on the heated griddle, cook until the top surface changes color to dryness (watch the surface and you will see the evaporation, drying and a subtle color change). Turn over with a spatula and brush the cooked surface evenly with ghee. Let cook for one minute, turn over and coat the other side with oil. Turn once again and cook until both sides are golden brown and crisp. Serve hot or stack on a paper towel, let cool and place inside a Ziploc bag. Makes 10-12.

Chawal ka Paratha (Rice Paratha)

1 cup rice flour
1 cup boiled & mashed potatoes
1 teaspoon salt
½ teaspoon cayenne pepper
1 teaspoon serrano pepper, finely chopped
1 tablespoon water

Mix all ingredients and make dough. Follow directions for paratha. Makes 6 parathas.

Dal ka Paratha (Lentil Paratha)

1 cup moong dal (hulled mung beans)
3¼ cups aata (whole wheat chapati flour)
1½ teaspoons ajwain
1 teaspoon kala jeera (caraway or black cumin)
3 teaspoons salt
½ teaspoon fennel seeds
½ teaspoon cayenne pepper
2-3 teaspoons oil
1 teaspoon garam masala
2 teaspoons cilantro, finely chopped
1½ cups water

Soak moong dal for 5 to 6 hours. Drain well. In a mixing bowl, mix flour, moong dal, ajwain, kala jeera, salt, saunf, cayenne pepper, oil, garam masala and chopped cilantro.

Make soft dough with water. Set aside for 30 minutes or more. Divide dough into 15 to 20 balls. Roll each ball into a 5 to 6 inch disc. On a heated griddle, shallow fry till crisp.

Serve hot. Makes 15 to 20 parathas.

Variation
The water may be reduced and a firm dough made. Roll out like pooris and deep fry.

Jeera Shahi Paratha

2 cups plain flour
1 cup aata (whole wheat flour)
2 teaspoons salt (adjust to taste)
1 teaspoon jeera (cumin seeds)
1 teaspoon cumin powder
1 teaspoon cayenne pepper (adjust to taste)
1 teaspoon black pepper
1 tablespoon ghee or melted butter
1 cup yogurt
¼ cup warm milk
¼ cup ghee or oil for preparing and frying the parathas
¼ cup flour to dust while rolling the parathas

To make the dough

Mix flours, salt and spices in bowl. Add oil and rub with flour to disperse evenly. Blend yogurt and milk and add to the flour while mixing. Knead to make a soft dough. Coat the dough evenly with a few drops of oil. Cover with damp cloth and set aside for half an hour at room temperature. Knead again and divide into ten. Make balls (peras) cover with a damp cloth and place in the refrigerator for half an hour.

Method

Heat a griddle to medium heat. Remove dough balls (peras) from the refrigerator. Dust rolling surface with dry flour and roll out the peras into 6 inch discs. Sprinkle 2 teaspoon oil on the disc and spread it with a pastry brush or the back of a spoon. Fold one edge of the disc to the center and then fold the other edge over the first fold (3 layers) to make a rectangle. Fold top $1/3$ edge of the rectangle to the center and bring lower edge over it, making a 3 layer square. Roll again into a $1/8$ inch thick square. Place on the heated griddle, cook until the top surface changes color to dryness (watch the surface and you will see the evaporation and a subtle color change to dryness). Turn over with a flat-face spatula, brush the cooked surface evenly with ghee. Let cook for one minute, turn over and coat the other side with oil. Turn once again and cook until both sides are golden brown and crisp. Serve hot from the griddle with plain yogurt or mint raita. Can cook ahead and reheat on the griddle immediately before serving. Store up to one week in the refrigerator, and one month in the freezer. If frozen, thaw before reheating on the griddle. Makes 10.

Methi Shahi Paratha

Replace cumin powder, cayenne pepper, and black pepper with 1 tablespoon kasoori methi (dried fenugreek leaves, available in Indian grocery stores). The rest of the ingredients remain the same. Follow the above procedure.

Poori

3 cups aata (wheat chapatti flour)
2 teaspoons oil
1 cup water
Oil for frying

Place aata in a deep bowl. Make a well in the center and pour 2 teaspoons oil. Knead aata with water till dough is firm and smooth, brush with a little oil. Roll out dough between the palms into a smooth log. Divide into 24 pieces and make smooth dough balls. Roll each ball out to 4 or 5 inch disc, with a rolling pin. Heat oil in a wok or fryer on medium high. Slide a poori gently in the hot oil, one at a time. Press gently with a perforated spatula, turning over when golden and puffed. Drain on paper towels and keep aside. Makes 24.

Palak Poori *(Spinach Poori)*

½ cup thawed chopped spinach
2 to 3 tablespoons water
1 cup aata (wheat chapati flour)
½ teaspoon salt
¼ teaspoon cumin seeds

Puree spinach with water. Mix flour and the spices. Make dough with pureed spinach.

Follow directions for poori. Makes 8.

Tomato Poori

1 cup aata (wheat chapatti flour)
6 tablespoons tomato sauce
¼ teaspoon cayenne pepper

Make stiff dough. Follow directions for pooris. Makes 8.

Bhatura

Indian immigrants, went to British Guiana as indentured labor settling there as 'The Bake'. Despite acquiring a new identity this recipe has survived cross-cultural exchanges, mergers of customs, traditions and intermarriages.

This recipe was shared with me by a third generation, multi-ethnic, Guiana-born naturalized citizen of America.

4 cups all purpose flour
2 tablespoons baking powder
½ stick butter
1 ½ cups plus 2 tablespoons tap water

Mix all the above ingredients and knead well into a dough. Use dry flour to handle the dough while kneading. Cover the dough with flour and paper towel. Let stand for ¾ hours. Roll out flat and deep fry on high heat, like puris. Serve immediately with Alu Cholle for best taste. Makes 12.

In Guiana "Bake" was served with honey like the Mexican Sopapia or powder sugar like the French beignets. This dough may be used for making Sopapia or beignets.

Masala Dosa *(Rice and Lentil Crepes with Potato Filling)*

Making dosa is an art and can be done with a lot of practice. Making a very thin crunchy crêpe requires batter of appropriate consistency, proper temperature of the griddle and a dexterity of hand to spread the batter.

1 ½ cups urad dal
3 cups long grain rice
½ cup poha (flattened rice) or plain, cooked rice
1 tablespoon methi seeds
Stick of butter, frozen

Potato Stuffing for Masala Dosa

6 large potatoes, boiled, peeled and cubed
2 tablespoons oil
1 teaspoon mustard seeds
1 tablespoon urad dal
15 kari leaves
2 medium sliced onions
1 inch ginger, chopped
6 hot green chili peppers, chopped
1 teaspoon turmeric
1 packet (10-ounce)frozen peas (optional)
1 tablespoon lemon juice
Salt to taste

Preparing the Dosa

Wash and soak rice and methi seeds. Wash and soak urad dal. Soak for 6 hours. Using a small amount of water, grind rice and dal separately, to a fine consistency. Wash poha and grind it fine. Put ground items in a large pot, and ferment in a warm place, overnight or until it doubles in volume. Dilute the mixture to pancake batter consistency and whisk it. Heat griddle to 350 to 400°F. The griddle is ready when a drop of water sizzles and evaporates. Pour a ladle of batter on the griddle. Using the back of the ladle or a flat bottom bowl spread the batter thin, like a crepe. Rub the surface with butter, flip and serve when brown. For masala dosa add 2 tablespoons filling in the center and fold both sides over the filling. Serve with coconut chutney and hot sambhar.

Filling

Heat oil in a wok over medium high heat. Add mustard seeds, kari leaves and urad dal. Stir, add onions, ginger, pepper, turmeric and peas. Mix well, Add potatoes, salt and lemon juice. Cover and simmer for few minutes. Garnish with chopped cilantro, if desired.

Proper fermentation is necessary to make a good dosa. Wipe the griddle with a wet paper towel after removing each dosa.

Multigrain Poora / Chilla *(Multigrain Crepes)*

Kheer- Poora is a coveted combination during the monsoon season. A slight Tamilian twist to the Punjabi Poora gives this monsoon delight a touch of north-south fusion. It makes a great breakfast or teatime tantalizer. Eat it with butter or yogurt and chunks of gur, (Jaggery) or serve with coconut chutney.

1 cup chapatti flour
1 cup makki ka atta
1 cup besan
2 teaspoon salt
½ cup finely chopped onion
2 teaspoon finely chopped chili pepper
¼ teaspoon red chili powder
¼ teaspoon cumin seed
Water
Oil to grease the griddle (tawa)

Mix all the ingredients in a large bowl. Add enough water to make a batter, slightly thinner than a pancake batter. Heat griddle, rub with a few drops of oil and check for the readiness of the griddle by sprinkling water over the hot griddle. If the water sputters makes a brisk sound and evaporates immediately, the griddle is ready. This is important for success in making pooras. Pour 3-4 tablespoons batter in the center of the griddle and spread into a thin circle, 7-8 inches in diameter. Turn over when the top appears slightly dry. Sprinkle a few drops of oil around and on the poora and turn once again. The poora should be speckled and golden brown. It should not have any burn marks. Makes 6-8.

Rice is grown extensively in Southern India and in the foothills of the Himalayas. The fertile Himalayan soil nurtures and nourishes the crop enhancing its flavor and aroma. Several kinds of rice are grown in India. The most well known is Basmati ("QUEEN OF FRAGRANCE") rice. It is a long grained, fragrant rice with low starch and is well suited for pulaos and biryanis or can be cooked plain.

Rice is also used in dessert such as rice kheer, and firni. Ground rice is used to thicken gravies and in batters to give it a crisp coating.

Rice should always be washed and drained prior to using. In Indian cooking, rice is either served plain or as a pulao or biryani. Plain rice may be seasoned with just salt and butter or oil. Pulaos (pulav, pilaf) can have many ingredients; whole spices, vegetables and nuts are usually included. The choice is endless and the selection depends on what is going to accompany it. Biryanis are usually cooked rice mixed with cooked meat or poultry and slow cooked to enhance the flavors, a signature dish from Mughlai cuisine.

Plain Rice

1 cup basmati rice
2 cups water
1 teaspoon salt (optional)
1 teaspoon butter (optional)

Wash the rice and drain it. In a 1½ quart saucepan add rice, water, salt and butter.

Bring to a boil, stirring a couple of times to prevent rice from sticking to the bottom of the pan. Lower heat to simmer and cover with a lid after a minute and cook for 12 to 15 minutes. Do not remove lid or stir during this time. Fluff rice and serve.

Cooked rice freezes well. Leftover rice can be used to make lemon rice (see receipe)

Carrot Pilaf

This rice has a beautiful orange hue and a slightly sweet taste. The addition of anise gives it a subtle flavor.

1 cup basmati rice
2 tablespoons ghee
 or 1 tablespoon butter and 1 tablespoon oil
¼ teaspoon anise or fennel seeds (saunf)
½ cup cashews
¼ cup raisins
1 teaspoon salt
2 cups water
2 carrots, peeled and coarsely grated (1 cup grated)

Wash and drain the rice. Heat ghee or butter and oil mixture in a 1 or 2-quart saucepan over moderate heat. Add anise and rice and sauté for about 3 minutes till rice appears opaque. Add cashews, raisins and salt. Add water and sprinkle carrots on top. When it comes to a boil, reduce heat to simmer and cover tightly. Cook for 15 minutes.

Fluff rice before serving.

One can use salted cashews from the supermarket; decrease salt to ½ teaspoon. Regular or golden raisins may be used. Other vegetables, such as sautéed sliced onions, mushrooms and peas may be substituted for the carrots.

Chicken Biryani

6 ½ tablespoons oil, divided
3 large onions, divided, finely chopped
2 cloves garlic, grated
1 tablespoon grated ginger
½ teaspoon cayenne pepper
½ teaspoon ground black pepper
½ teaspoon turmeric
1 teaspoon black cumin seeds
1 teaspoon salt
2 medium tomatoes, finely chopped
2 tablespoons plain yogurt
2 tablespoons, fresh mint leaves, finely chopped
2 tablespoons fresh cilantro leaves, finely chopped
½ teaspoon ground cardamom
2 sticks cinnamon
2 ½ pounds boneless and skinless chicken, cut into chunks
1 pinch saffron
4 whole cardamom pods
4 cloves
2 cups (1 pound) basmati rice
4 cups hot chicken stock
1 ½ teaspoons salt

In a large skillet add 4 tablespoons oil and fry 2/3 of the onions, garlic and ginger until onions are soft and golden. Add cayenne pepper, black pepper, turmeric, black cumin seeds, salt and tomatoes. Fry, stirring constantly for 5 minutes. Add yogurt, mint, cilantro, cardamom and 1 cinnamon stick. Cover and cook over low heat, stirring occasionally until the tomatoes are cooked to a pulp. It may be necessary to add a little hot water if the mixture becomes too dry and starts sticking to the pan. When the mixture is thick and smooth, add chicken pieces and stir well to coat them with the spice mixture. Cover and cook over very low heat until the chicken is tender (approximately 25 to 30 minutes). A little thick gravy should remain when chicken is cooked. If necessary, cook uncovered for a few minutes to reduce the gravy.

Wash rice well and drain in a colander for at least 30 minutes. In a large skillet, heat 2 tablespoons oil (or ghee) and fry remaining onion until golden. Add saffron, cardamom pods, cloves, 1 cinnamon stick and rice. Sauté until rice is coated with the spices for about 5 minutes. Add hot chicken stock and salt. Stir well and add chicken mixture; gently mixing it into the rice. Bring to a boil. Then cover the saucepan tightly, turn heat to very low and steam for 20 minutes. Do not lift lid during this time. Serve hot. Total cooking time: 1 hour. Serves 4 to 6.

*Hakeemi** Zarda Sweet Rice

Bebe ji (grand mother) served this TLC vapor to provide relief from discomfort of common cold. She would set a cot out in the sun, tuck the sufferer under a blanket, covered from head to toe, grandma's version of a sauna, then slide a large bowl of steaming rice through a peep hole. You had to inhale deeply for at least 15 minutes. You would start eating only after the steam calmed down. You did not dare to peek until all the rice was eaten. Guess what? Although we used to fuss and complain, that was not hard at all! The rice was delicious and instant relief from the stuffiness.

1 cup rice
1 ½ cups water
1 teaspoon cumin seeds
1 tablespoon ghee
1 cup sugar
½ cup milk, boiling hot
½ teaspoon yellow food color

Melt ghee in a pan. Add cumin seed and let them crackle. Add rice and stir-fry (bhuno) for 1 minute. Add water and bring to boil. Cook on medium heat for 12 to14 minutes. Now dissolve sugar and food color in boiled milk, pour sugar mixture over partially cooked rice and cook for 7 to 10 minutes. Serve piping hot.

Hakeem   Medicine man
*Hakeemi   Of the Medicine man

Jeera Rice Pilaf

2 cups basmati rice, washed and drained
1 onion, finely sliced
1 tablespoon oil
½ teaspoon cumin seeds
3 ½ cups water
1 teaspoon salt
½ cup frozen sweet peas, thawed (optional)
1 tablespoon butter

Heat a 2-quart saucepan on high heat and add oil and cumin seeds. Stir for 30 seconds to release aroma. Lower heat to medium; add onions and fry till golden brown for about 5 minutes. Add rice and stir to coat rice with oil. When rice turns translucent in 2-3 minutes, add water and salt and bring to a boil. Add peas, cover the pan tightly and simmer on lowest heat for 20 minutes. Add butter and fluff rice with a fork and transfer to a serving dish. Serve hot. Serves 8.

Harmony Rice Pilaf

This recipe won the "Kitchen Queen" prize in the food competition at the international festival at Louisiana State University in 1992. It has been popular with the children ever since.

1 cup basmati rice
2 cups water
2 tablespoons oil
1 onion, finely chopped
¼ teaspoon cumin seeds
4 cloves
1 cinnamon stick
1 cup mixed vegetables
1 teaspoon salt
1 teaspoon garam masala
¼ cup raisins
¼ cup cashews
2 tablespoons lemon juice

Wash rice and soak in 2 cups of water for 15 minutes.

Heat oil in a sauté pan over moderate heat. Sauté onions till they become brownish. Add cumin seeds, cloves and cinnamon stick and stir for 30 seconds. Add mixed vegetables (thaw, if using frozen), salt, garam masala, raisins and cashews. Mix these ingredients well and add rice and water and bring to a boil on high heat. Lower heat to simmer and cover tightly. Cook for about 10 minutes. When all the water is absorbed add lemon juice. Serve with plain yogurt. Serves 4-5.

Other vegetables such as green peas, carrots, green beans, corn, diced tomatoes, bell pepper etc. may be substituted for mixed vegetables.

Khichdi Jamai ji *(Rice and Lentil Casserole)*

Khichdi is a mixture of dal and rice that is cooked together so that the flavors blend together. Various lentils can be used, such as split moong dal with or without skin, whole brown lentils (*masoor*) or *moath* lentils. It can be made with or without the addition of any number of vegetables. The proportion of rice to lentils also varies with individuals. Khichdi is often served with four accompaniments; papadams, yogurt, ghee, and pickles. This recipe is a meal in itself and a favorite of the son-in law.

¾ cup basmati rice
¾ cup split moong dal with skin, picked over
2 tablespoons ghee or vegetable oil
¾ teaspoon cumin seeds
1/8 teaspoon asafetida (hing)
2 dried red chilies
4 cloves
1-inch piece cinnamon stick
1-2 bay leaves
1 large black cardamom
3 ¼ cups water
½ teaspoon turmeric
2 teaspoons salt
1 medium potato, peeled and diced
½-¾ cup frozen green peas

Rinse rice and moong beans thrice with water and set aside. In a 2 or 3-quart saucepan, heat ghee or oil over medium heat. Add cumin seeds & when they begin to sizzle, add asafetida, red chilies, cloves, cinnamon, bay leaf and cardamom. Sauté for about 30 seconds to release the flavor of the spices. Add the rice and bean mixture, water, turmeric, salt, potatoes and peas. Stir, bring to a boil, and then turn the heat to simmer. Stir the mixture once again, cover and cook approximately for 15 minutes or until water has been absorbed. Remove whole spices before serving. Serve with papadams, plain yogurt and lime, mango or chili pickle.

Lemon Rice

This recipe is a wonderful way to use up leftover rice from the night before. If the rice has been refrigerated, heat it in a microwave to warm and soften the rice prior to using it. Or cook 1 cup plain rice and allow to cool before proceeding with the recipe.

4 cups cooked basmati or other long grain rice
4 tablespoons vegetable oil
1 teaspoon mustard seeds
1/8 teaspoon asafetida (hing)
2-3 dried red chilies
6-8 kari leaves
1/2 cup cashew pieces (optional)
1 cup chopped onion
1/2 teaspoon turmeric (haldi)
1 teaspoon salt
Juice of 1 lemon or lime
Zest of 1 lemon or lime, optional

Heat oil in a large sauté pan over moderate heat. Add mustard seeds and asafetida. When mustard seeds begin to splutter (about 30 seconds) add red chilies, kari leaves and cashews. Sauté for 15 seconds till the cashews are roasted. Add onions and cook until pink. Add turmeric and rice. Sprinkle salt over rice, mix well, but gently so that oil and spices coat the rice. Add lemon juice and rind. Turn heat to low. Cover and cook for a few more minutes until the rice is hot. Serve with any hot pickle as a main dish for brunch, lunch or as a side rice dish with western meals.

Optional: One can add 1 teaspoon of urad dal and 1 teaspoon of chana dal when the mustard seeds change color. Sauté for 15 seconds till they turn light brown.

Peas Pulao *(Microwave Method)*

Rice can be cooked easily in a microwave. However, remember that as wattage varies with different microwaves adjust time to cook according.

1 cup basmati rice, washed and drained
1 cup frozen green peas, thawed
1 or 2 serrano peppers, chopped
2 cinnamon sticks
2 cloves
2-3 bay leaves
2 tablespoons oil
2¼ cups warm water
1 teaspoon salt, or to taste

Put oil in a microwavable bowl and heat on high for 15 seconds. Add cinnamon, cloves, bay leaves and serrano peppers and microwave again for about 2 minutes (stirring once in between for a few seconds). Add rice, green peas, 2 ¼ cup warm water and salt, cover and microwave for about 10 minutes on high heat (stirring once in between after about 5 minutes). Rice is done when water is absorbed completely. Serve hot with any curry.

Shrimp Pilaf

2-3 pounds large shrimp
2 cups basmati rice, washed and drained
3 cups water
2 large onions, finely sliced
1 teaspoon salt
2 tablespoon ginger, grated
½ teaspoon turmeric powder
1 tablespoon butter
½ cup vegetable oil
2 cinnamon sticks
8 whole cloves
8 whole cardamoms pods
8 peppercorns
2 bay leaves
Few fresh cilantro leaves (for garnishing)

Clean shrimp, leaving the tails intact. Rinse out in cold water and pat dry. Mix with turmeric and salt. Heat oil in a skillet. Sauté shrimp until color changes. Remove from heat. Using the same oil, sauté onions. Add rice, salt, ginger, turmeric powder, butter, cinnamon, cloves, cardamom, peppercorns and bay leaves. Stir over medium heat. When rice looks opaque, add water and bring to a boil. Cover and simmer for 10 to 12 minutes. Put in the shrimp and mix well. Keep covered but turn the heat off. Garnish with cilantro before serving. Serve hot.

Serves 4 to 6.

Sasur ji Delight Pulau

¼ cup sliced onion sautéed in 2 tablespoons oil
2 cups basmati rice
1 teaspoon cumin seeds
2 tablespoons butter
1 teaspoon turmeric
2 teaspoons salt
1 teaspoon cayenne pepper
1 teaspoon freshly ground black pepper
4 cups water
1 package (14 oz) frozen spinach, cooked as per direction
½ cup grape tomatoes

Combine first 9 ingredients (everything except spinach and tomatoes) in a 6-quart pot. Bring water to boil. Cover and simmer for 18 minutes. Add cooked spinach and whole grape tomatoes. Continue to cook for another 2-3 minutes. Let stand for 5 minutes. Mix and serve piping hot. Serves 10-15.

Beverages

Hot Chocolate *By Congressman Bobby Jindal*

Sometimes it's the smallest things that stay with you forever. Some of my brightest childhood memories center around memories of making hot chocolate with my grandfather. I idolized him; he was the first true hero in my life.

It may seem trivial, but one of the things that made our relationship special was the hot chocolate. A simple hot drink that allowed me to learn so much about family, life, and love. Grandpa would keep me entertained with tales from his childhood, and I would sit transfixed in the kitchen chair. He seemed so wise, even to a young child like me.

I remember the first time he let me help make the hot chocolate. I, as any child would have, made a giant mess. Cocoa powder everywhere, water everywhere—you name it, I managed to make a mess of it. But Grandpa didn't get mad, he just laughed. These early times in my life with my grandfather helped shape me into the man I am today. I can only hope to pass on the same love, strength, and patience to my children and grandchildren. You can believe that in my attempts to do so, I will be doing it with cups of hot chocolate.

1 and 2/3 cups warm water
4 and 2/3 oz. can sweetened condensed milk
1/5 cup unsweetened cocoa powder
1/2 teaspoon vanilla extract
1/16 teaspoon salt

Combine all ingredients in a 2-quart saucepan and warm over medium heat, or combine all ingredients in a 4-cup microwave-safe bowl and heat in the microwave, for 6-8 minutes. Stir every 1 1/2 minutes.

Add marshmallows to taste.

Mango Lassi

A lassi is a shake made with yogurt or buttermilk. Most often it is sweetened with sugar. It can also be flavored with different essences. Lassi can also be salty.

1 can (30-ounce) mango pulp, preferably chilled
Equal amount of buttermilk (preferably Country Bulgarian Style)
1½ cups ice cubes
⅓ cup sugar or ⅓ cup Splenda

Mix all ingredients together in a blender and serve chilled in tall glasses. May be diluted by adding water and sweetened by adding sugar as desired. Can also be made in advance of a meal. Stir prior to serving. Mango lassi may be served as a drink or with a meal.

Mangosa

2 (1-quart) bottles Maaza or other mango drink
1 (2-quart) bottle Sprite, or other lime and lemon soda, chilled
1 (750 ml) bottle champagne, chilled

Mix equal amounts of chilled mango drink with Sprite. Pour half full in tall glasses. Fill the glass with chilled champagne. Serve at once.

Makes a good punch for a wedding shower or a summer brunch

Variations

Use equal amounts of mango drink and Sprite and omit the champagne

Use equal amounts of mango drink and champagne and omit the Sprite.

Mango Panna *(Raw Mango Cooler)*

This is a favorite drink during early summer when raw mangoes are in season. The tartness of raw mango gives the drink its unique flavor. Purchase these mangoes at Asian grocery stores.

1 large unripe mango (1 pound)
4 cups iced water
1 ¼ cups sugar
1/8 to ¼ teaspoon citric acid crystals
Salt to taste
½ teaspoon cumin seeds, roasted and ground

Peel mango and cut into thick slices. Cook mango slices in a small saucepan with 2 cups of water for about 20 minutes or until soft. Alternatively, cook in a pressure cooker; adding 1 cup of water to the bottom of the pressure cooker and 1 cup of water in a small pan in which the mango is placed. Cook for 1 whistle; when pressure builds up turn off the heat and allow pressure to drop on its own. Puree the cooked mango in a blender; add 4 cups of iced water. Add slightly more than 1 cup of sugar, depending on the tartness of the mango. Add salt and roasted cumin powder. Taste the drink and add citric acid to make it more tart if the mango is bland. The drink should be greenish-yellow in color, slightly thick, with a sweet and sour taste with a touch of salt. Serve chilled serves 4.

The pulp may be made in a larger quantity and refrigerated in an airtight container for several days. Dilute as needed.

Masala Chai Latte

½ cup water
½ cup milk
$1/8$ teaspoon tea masala (chai masala)
1 tea bag or 1 teaspoon loose tea leaves
Sugar or sweetener, to taste

In a saucepan bring cold water to a boil. Add tea and tea masala. Turn heat off and steep tea for 3 minutes. Heat milk. Mix equal parts tea and milk and sweeten to taste.

Can be served hot or cold over crushed ice.

Masala Milk *(Saffron Milk Punch)*

8 ounces milk (whole or low fat)

1 teaspoon nut masala

1-2 teaspoons sugar, to taste or 1-2 packets Splenda

Mix nut masala and sugar with milk

Masala

1 cup raw almonds

½ cup unsalted pistachios

3 teaspoons green cardamom seeds, powdered

1 teaspoon saffron threads, powdered

Grind almonds and pistachios in a coffee grinder to a fine powder. Add cardamom and saffron powder to the nut mixture and mix well. Makes 1 ¾ cup masala mixture.

To make a larger quantity add ⅓ cups masala to 2 quarts (8 cups) milk. Refrigerate for an hour or more to blend flavors. Stir just before serving. Can also be prepared at night for breakfast in the morning breakfast in the morning. Store in an airtight jar in the refrigerator. Will keep for 4 months or longer.

This is a versatile masala and can be used in rice kheer, burfi and other desserts.
Pick pistachios to remove any that are not fresh. Unsalted pistachios become rancid fast. Store in the freezer. The proportion of almonds to pistachios, and amount of cardamom and saffron can be adusted to ones taste. Too much saffron imparts a bitter taste and a dark yellow color. Cardamom and saffron can be ground fine with a mortar and pestle or with the nuts in a coffee grinder. Do not over process the nuts otherwise they become oily.

Pineapple Ginger Cooler

1 can (46-ounce) pineapple juice
1 tablespoon fresh ginger juice
1 ½ tablespoons fresh lemon juice
3 teaspoons black salt
1 teaspoon salt
1 can (12-ounce) Sprite or Ginger ale
1-2 teaspoons mint, crushed or finely chopped
½ lemon, very finely sliced

Mix pineapple, ginger and lemon juices and black and regular salt in a large jug.

Add Sprite and mint and stir. Put lemon slices on top. Serve over crushed ice in tall glasses. Makes a very refreshing teatime punch

May use 2 tablespoons of crushed ginger and allow it to steep in the pineapple juice. Strain before pouring the juice.

Punjabi Lassi

The Northern State of Punjab is the agricultural heartland of India. Milk and milk products such as yogurt and paneer are available in plenty. Lassi is a favorite drink at home as well as neighborhood shops selling dairy products.

1 quart whole milk plain yogurt
2 cups cold water
½ cup sugar or equal amount of Splenda
8 drops Kevda essence

Blend all ingredients together to make a thick shake. Serve in a cold tall glass.

One of the following can also be used to flavor lassi instead of Kevda essence:-

1 teaspoon rosewater
1/8 teaspoon ground cardamom
1 tablespoon Rooh afza

Spicy Melon Cooler

This cooler is a refreshing change from the sweet fruit juices or punch one has in the summer.

½ Honey Dew melon, peeled & cut into chunks
1 cup water
½ teaspoon sugar
¼ teaspoon salt
Pinch of black salt
4 mint leaves
1-2 cilantro leaves
A thin sliver of fresh ginger, peeled
¼ teaspoon hot green chili pepper
Juice of one orange
2-3 drops lemon juice
Crushed ice

Blend melon chunks, water, sugar, salt, mint, cilantro, ginger and chili in a blender. Strain and add orange and lemon juice. Mix and serve over crushed ice.

Summer Melon Cooler

½ Cantaloupe melon, peeled and cut into chunks
1 cup water
¼ to ½ teaspoon sugar
Juice of 2 to 3 oranges
Few drops of fresh lemon juice
Crushed ice

Blend melon chunks, water and sugar in a blender. Strain and add orange and lemon juice. Mix and serve over crushed ice.

Tiger Punch

1 (48 ounce) can pineapple juice
1 (48 ounce) can apple juice
1 (2 litre) bottle of Sprite or any lime and lemon soda
5 mint leaves or 5 strawberries

The night before serving, place cans of pineapple and apple juice in the freezer. Take juices out of the freezer one hour before serving and set aside. Empty the juices into a punch bowl and pour Sprite over it. Garnish with mint leaves or strawberries for color. Other sliced fruits may be used for garnishing.

Watermelon Smoothie

A beautiful pale pink refreshing drink that perfectly compliments spicy breakfast dishes such as upma and poha.

4 cups watermelon
2 cups milk
3 tablespoons sugar or to taste
7-8 ice cubes

Remove the seeds from watermelon and cut into large cubes. In a blender add melon cubes, milk, sugar and ice. Blend on high for about a minute. Serve immediately, chilled in tall glasses. Garnish with a thin slice of watermelon or a sprig of mint.

If made in advance, stir before serving as liquid will separate and solids will settle down. Serves 2-3.

Spice Box

Chutneys and Dressings

Pickles, raita, chutney and papads usually accompany an Indian meal.

Pickles are very popular in India. They are served with all kinds of vegetarian and non-vegetarian dishes at every meal. They generally fall into three categories: sweet, hot and sweet/sour. Some pickles are made fresh and kept in the refrigerator. Most of them are made with seasonal fruits and vegetables and contain oil, salt and spices, which act as a preservative. The variety of pickles in the Indian grocery store is enormous. Some are also available in supermarkets. We have an appetizer recipe for Chunda, a sweet and sour mango pickle over cream cheese in this book.

Raitas are usually a combination of yogurt with fruits, vegetables and spices. Cucumber, mint, tomato and onion, broccoli, spinach, pumpkin, squash can all be used for raitas. Some are grated raw, while others are cooked and mixed in the yogurt. Apples, bananas and oranges can also be used. Traditionally, Taitas are served with all meals. These cool the palate.

Chutneys are relishes of Indian cuisine. They are usually eaten in small amounts and add great flavor to the meal. In India, a chutney is customarily made on a grinding stone on which ingredients are ground to a fine paste. Some chutneys are chunky, while others are cooked and chilled prior to serving. Chutneys are also available in bottles in Indian grocery stores.

Papadums or **Papads** are thin wafers generally made from powdered lentils. These are commonly spiced with cumin, cayenne or black pepper. They may be roasted in a microwave oven (recipe given) or on a gas flame. They can also be deep fried in very hot oil. Small sago wafers are usually deep-fried. These can be purchased from any Indian grocery store.

Coconut Chutney

Coconut is widely used in South Indian cooking. Fresh chutneys are ground daily in homes in India and served in small quantities as a condiment with all meals. The word chutney is derived from the Indian word "chaatnaa" which means "to lick".

2 packages (6-ounce) frozen unsweetened coconut , thawed
2 hot green chili peppers
2 tablespoons ginger, peeled and chopped
1½ cups warm water
Salt to taste
1 cup plain yogurt
1 teaspoon lemon juice
Tadka
1 tablespoon oil
½ teaspoon mustard seeds
½ teaspoon split and skinned urad dal (optional)
4-5 kari leaves
1 whole dried red chili

Grind coconut, green chilies and ginger in a blender with water. Whisk in salt and yogurt. Heat oil in a small pan; add mustard seeds, urad dal, hot chili, pepper & kari leaves. When mustard seeds begin to pop remove pan from heat and pour over the chutney. Serve at room temperature with vada, idli or dosas. Makes about 3 cups.

Frozen unsweetened coconut is available in the freezer section of your local supermarket and Indian stores. Use of warm water to grind is necessary to prevent the coconut cream from separating. The chutney remains fresh for 1 week in the refrigerator and can also be frozen.

Garlic Chutney

This is a very spicy blend of garlic and cayenne. Be careful when tasting it!

1 bulb (not clove) garlic, peeled
1 red bell pepper, seeded and chopped
1 tablespoon cayenne pepper
1 tablespoon coriander powder
½ tablespoon cumin powder
1 teaspoon salt
Juice of one lemon

Place all ingredients in a blender or food processor and process to a fine puree. Store covered in the refrigerator or freeze for later use. Serve with hot pakoras. For use in bhel, dilute 2 tablespoons chutney with ½ cup water.

Mithi Chutney *(Date Chutney)*

This sweet and sour chutney is used extensively in the cuisine of Gujarat State. It is an integral part of bhel.

1 cup pitted dates
2 teaspoons tamarind paste
1 teaspoon salt or black salt (available in Indian grocery stores)
½ teaspoon cumin seeds
½ teaspoon cayenne pepper
1 tablespoon sugar
2 tablespoons lemon juice
2¼ cups water

Mix all the ingredients in a blender or food processor. Process on high speed until it forms a smooth puree. Can be stored in an airtight container in the refrigerator up to 1 week. Serve with bhel, samosas, kachoris or other chaat items.

Kerala Tomato Chutney

The food from South India is generally hotter than North India because of the amount of cayenne pepper used. The amount of Serrano peppers used here may be adjusted to taste. This chutney complements the bland idlis (rice and lentil dumplings) and dosas (rice and lentil crepes) of Southern India.

2 Roma tomatoes
2 shallots or ¼ onion, finely chopped
2 hot green chili peppers
2 tablespoons fresh coconut, grated
Or (desiccated coconut soaked in 3 tablespoons water for 5 minutes)
1 teaspoon fresh ginger, grated
3 teaspoons oil, divided
¼ teaspoon mustard seeds
6-8 kari leaves
½ teaspoon salt, or to taste

Sauté whole tomatoes with 1 teaspoon oil in a small skillet for 2 to 3 minutes. Keep aside. To the skillet add 1 teaspoon oil, shallots or onions and 3 or 4 kari leaves. Sauté for 1 to 2 minutes until onion is cooked. Grind chili peppers, coconut and ginger in a blender. Add sautéed tomato and onion mixture and grind to a paste. Transfer mixture to a small serving bowl. Heat 1 teaspoon oil in a small skillet over medium heat. Add mustard seeds and 3 or 4 kari leaves. When mustard seeds begin to pop, remove from heat and pour over the tomato mixture. Mix and serve at room temperature. Makes 1 cup.

Mint Chutney

A popular chutney that can be served with pakoras or samosas. Use a thin layer with butter or cream cheese as a spread for cucumber sandwiches. Lime-juice enhances the flavor of mint and cilantro and helps to retain the green color.

1 bunch mint leaves
1 bunch cilantro
1 hot green chili pepper, chopped
1 medium onion, chopped
¼ cup green peas
1 clove garlic, peeled
2 tablespoons lime juice
Salt, to taste
Basil leaves (optional)

Wash mint and cilantro. Put all ingredients in a blender or food processor and grind to a thick paste. Add a handful of basil leaves to give chutney a complex flavor.

Substitute 1 tablespoon vinegar for lime juice to keep the chutney fresh for several weeks in the refrigerator.

Hot and Sweet Cranberry Chutney

1 (12-ounce) packet fresh cranberries, washed and dried
1 teaspoon fenugreek seeds (methi)
½ teaspoon asafetida powder (hing)
¼ cup olive oil
1 tablespoon salt or to taste
1 ½ tablespoons cayenne pepper
4 tablespoons brown sugar
1 teaspoon mustard seeds

In a small skillet, dry roast fenugreek seeds till they turn brown. Add asafetida powder and roast for a few seconds more. Cool and grind to a fine powder. Keep aside.

Heat olive oil in a heavy bottomed pan, over medium heat. Add mustard seeds. When seeds begin to pop, add cranberries and sauté for 10 to 15 minutes until soft. Add salt and sauté for 2 more minutes. Add cayenne and sauté for another 2 minutes.

Remove pan from heat and add powdered fenugreek seeds and stir well. Add brown sugar and stir. Brown sugar may be omitted or increased depending on individual taste.

Sweet and Sour Fruit Chutney

Fruit chutneys are a good accompaniment to pork, roasted chicken or turkey. Any single fruit or a combination of several fruits such as peaches, plums, prunes, pineapples, cherries, strawberries, cranberries, oranges or crab apples, can be used.

1 tablespoon vegetable oil
¼ teaspoon mustard seeds
¼ teaspoon turmeric
4 apples, peeled, cored and sliced
1 (15-ounce) can whole tomatoes or 6 fresh tomatoes, chopped
½ teaspoon fresh ginger, peeled and grated
1 teaspoon salt
1-2 teaspoons cinnamon powder or 1 (3-inch) cinnamon stick
½ cup sugar (honey or molasses)
1 pound raisins
½ cup water (or canned fruit juice)
2 tablespoons lemon juice
Pinch of cayenne pepper

Heat oil in a large saucepan. Add mustard seeds and cover. When mustard seeds begin to pop, add turmeric, apples and tomatoes (or just the juice, if using canned tomatoes). Sauté for a minute & add ginger, salt, cinnamon, sugar and raisins. Add water (or drained tomatoes) and lemon juice. Cook over low heat until thick (15 to 20 minutes). Serve when cool, adding a dash of cayenne, if desired.

Zesty Cilantro Chutney

1 bunch cilantro, cleaned and washed
1 large onion, peeled and cut into quarters
2 tablespoons lemon juice
2 tablespoons peanuts
1-inch fresh ginger, peeled and chopped
2 hot green chili peppers
1 teaspoon salt

Mix all the ingredients in a blender and grind to a fine paste.

Serve with pakoras, samosas, aloo tikki or bhel.

Tomato Curry / Chutney

2 large tomatoes, sliced
OR
1 (15-ounce) can chopped tomatoes
1 ½ tablespoons oil
½ teaspoon cumin seeds*
½ teaspoon mustard seeds*
½ teaspoon fennel seeds*
½ teaspoon nigella seeds*
½ teaspoon fenugreek seeds*
1 bay leaf
½ inch piece ginger, peeled and grated
1 hot green chili pepper, sliced
1 teaspoon salt
1 teaspoon cayenne pepper
¼ teaspoon turmeric
1 teaspoon coriander powder
2 to 3 tablespoons sugar
2 tablespoons chopped cilantro to garnish

Heat oil in a 3-quart saucepan over medium heat. Add cumin, mustard, fennel, nigella and fenugreek seeds (or panch phoran) and bay leaf. When mustard seeds begin to pop, add ginger and green chili peppers. Stir once and add tomatoes. Stir for a few seconds, add salt, cayenne pepper, turmeric and coriander powder. Mix well and lower heat to medium. Cover and cook for 10 minutes or till tomatoes become soft. Add sugar and cook for an additional 2 minutes. Garnish with chopped cilantro. Tomato Curry/Chutney can be served as a relish or a vegetable with rotis or rice.

Substitute 2 ½ teaspoons of panch phoran for these 5 ingredients

Cilantro Vinaigrette

This is a fresh dressing that is easy to make and adds a unique taste to your salad.

½ cup chopped cilantro
Juice of ½ a lemon
1 teaspoon sugar or 1 packet artificial sweetener
½ teaspoon salt
Freshly ground black pepper, to taste
¼ cup extra virgin olive oil

Mix cilantro, lemon juice, sugar or artificial sweetener, salt and black pepper in a glass bowl. Using a whisk, add olive oil in a steady stream and whisk until all the oil is incorporated in the dressing. Adjust salt and pepper to taste. Serve over salad greens or with chicken tikka. Makes ½ cup dressing. Mint, Basil and Terragon can be substituted for Cilantro for a refreshing flavor.

Garam Masala

1 cup coriander seeds
2 cups cumin seeds
¼ cup cloves
1/8 cup cinnamon sticks
1/8 cup green cardamom
1/8 cup black cardamom
¼ cup black peppercorn
1 cup bay leaves

Lightly roast coriander seeds in a flat bottomed heavy pan until light brown. Remove.

Similarly roast each spice individually. Cool and grind in a coffee grinder. Makes 5 cups.

Suggestion

If Indian cooking is an infrequent adventure for you, share this masala with your friends.

Packed in a 6-ounce Mason jar with a cinnamon stick tied with a ribbon onto the lid. It makes a great gourmet gift.

Ammaji's Garam Masala

Garam means hot in Hindi and masala is a mixture. The traditional spices used in garam masala are cinnamon, cloves, black pepper and cardamom. The first 3 are called warm spices as they produce heat in the body. Cardamom is a cooling spice. One can customize this mixture by adding different spices for a secret family recipe.

Store bought garam masala is okay to substitute; Rajah brand is preferred. Store bought garam masala often has a larger quantity of cloves, making it strong. Addition of cumin and coriander seeds makes it milder.

½ cup cumin seeds
½ cup coriander seeds
1 tablespoon cloves
1 tablespoon black peppercorns
30 big black cardamoms
6 inches rolled cinnamon sticks
9 large bayleaves
1 teaspoon seeds from green cardamoms

Grind all ingredients together in a coffee grinder till finely powdered (do not roast the spices). Sift through a fine mesh sieve. Store in an airtight bottle in a cool cabinet. For optimum flavor use within 3 months. Spices lose their potency with time but garam masala may be used up to 1 year. Makes 1 cup.

Chai Masala (Tea Masala)

1 teaspoon powdered cinnamon powder
1 teaspoon or less powdered cloves
1 teaspoon powdered black pepper
1 teaspoon powdered dried ginger
2 teaspoons powdered green cardamom seeds

Mix all together and store in an airtight container.

Mint Dressing

2 tablespoon tarragon vinegar
1 teaspoon fresh lemon juice
1 tablespoon yogurt
4 teaspoons olive oil
2 cloves garlic, minced
½ teaspoon freshly ground black pepper
1 teaspoon salt
2 tablespoons mint leaves, finely chopped

In a small bowl whisk vinegar, lemon juice and yogurt together until smooth. Add oil and continue to whisk. Add garlic, black pepper and salt. Mix until salt is completely dissolved. Add mint leaves just prior to serving. Serve over fresh cucumber and lettuce salad.

Karela and Bhindi Masala

2 tablespoons fennel seeds
2 tablespoons coriander seeds
2 tablespoons cumin seeds
2 tablespoons pomegranate seeds
2 tablespoons mango powder
1 tablespoon black pepper
1 tablespoon garam masala
1 tablespoon methi seeds
1 tablespoon salt
1 ½ teaspoon turmeric(haldi)
1 teaspoon green dry methi powder (optional!)

Place all the ingredients in a spice (coffee) grinder and grind very fine. Pomegranate seeds will remain characteristically a bit granular and gritty but they will soften with cooking. Store in an air-tight container and use as needed. This masala may be used for okra, karela, or potatoes. Store in the refrigerator to preserve freshness.

Sambhar Masala

1 tablespoon cumin seeds
½ teaspoon coriander seeds
10 cloves
½ teaspoon cinnamon pieces
5 dry red chilies
1 teaspoon black peppercorns
4 bay leaves
1½ teaspoons fenugreek seeds (methi)
1½ teaspoons urad dal
3-inch piece khopra (dry coconut) chopped
1/8 teaspoon garam masala

Roast cumin, coriander, cloves, cinnamon, red chilies, black pepper and bay leaves together in a heavy pan on medium heat. Roast fenugreek seeds, urad dal and coconut separately. Grind all the roasted spices together in a coffee grinder. Mix well. Add garam masala and store in an airtight jar. Use as needed in sambhar, rasam or other dals.

Panch Phoran

1 teaspoon mustard seeds (rai)
1 teaspoon fenugreek seeds (methi)
1 teaspoon nigella seeds (kalonji)
1 teaspoon anise seeds (saunf)
1 teaspoon cumin seeds (jeera)

Mix all ingredients and store in a jar in a cool place. It is commonly used in the Bengali cuisine.

It is available in packets in Indian grocery stores.

Cranberry and Green Chili Pickle

This is a unique pickle that is tangy and hot. Do not substitute with frozen cranberries as their moisture content is too high.

24 ounces fresh cranberries
1 cup Serrano chili peppers, chopped in ¼ inch pieces
¼ cup ground yellow mustard seeds
¼ cup coarse ground fennel
1 tablespoon nigella seeds
¾ tablespoon cayenne pepper
3 teaspoons salt or to taste
2 cups oil, heated and then cooled
4 (pint size) Mason jars

Wash cranberries and Serrano peppers. Dry them well. (This is important!) Cut each cranberry in half. Mix all ingredients thoroughly. Spoon pickle in jars and add oil until it covers the top. Cap jars and leave in the sun for 1 day. Stored in the refrigerator the pickle will last for a couple of months.

Makes 4, pint-size jars.

Serrano peppers may be substituted with any hot green chilies. However, for a milder pickle omit Serrano peppers and reduce salt to 2 teaspoons.

Mango Potli Achar

10-12 pounds mango, peeled and grated
1 pound salt
2 cups each kalonji, saunf, red pepper and crushed black pepper
¼ cup turmeric powder
2 cups mustard oil

Mix the spices with oil and add grated mango. Mix well. Cut muslin cloth in 12 inches square pieces. Place 2 cups mixture in the center of the cloth and tie (potlies) with kitchen cord. Place these potlies in a jar. Add oil to cover, about an inch above the potlies. Keep the jar in full hot sun for 4-5 days. Remove one potly at a time and open onto a flat plate to serve. Tuck the corners under with a fork to make bubble edges. A great conversation piece.

Pineapple Pickle

Pineapple pickle is a good alternative to a vegetable and can be served along with hot puris and parathas. It is a good accompaniment to roasted pork, too.

1 ripe pineapple, peeled, cleaned and cut in 1- inch pieces
OR
3 (20-ounce) pineapple cans, chunk-style, drained well
3 tablespoons vegetable oil
1½ teaspoons mustard seeds
3 cloves garlic, peeled and shredded
1 inch piece fresh ginger, peeled and shredded
½ to 1 teaspoon cayenne pepper
2 teaspoons coriander powder
½ teaspoon cumin powder
¼ teaspoon turmeric
1½ teaspoons salt
3 teaspoons sugar
½ cup vinegar

Heat oil in a 3-inch deep, non-stick pan over medium heat. Add mustard seeds. When they begin to pop, add garlic and ginger. Sauté for 30 seconds. Reduce heat to low and add cayenne, coriander, cumin powder and turmeric. Sauté for 20 seconds. Add salt, sugar and vinegar. Stir and add the pineapple. Mix thoroughly, cover and simmer for 10 minutes. Do not add water. Canned pineapple takes longer to cook (about 15 minutes)

Serve at room temperature. To store this pickle in a refrigerator: Heat 1 cup oil and allow it to cool to room temperature. Place pickle in a jar and pour oil to cover.

Broccoli Raita

1 cup broccoli, finely chopped or grated
1 tablespoon oil
1 small onion, finely chopped
1 clove finely chopped garlic,
1 teaspoon finely chopped ginger
1 teaspoon salt
¼ teaspoon ground cloves
¼ teaspoon ground cinnamon
¼ teaspoon ground cardamom seeds
2 cups thick yogurt, whisked
For Tadka (optional)
1 teaspoon oil
4-5 whole cloves

Heat 1 tablespoon oil and sauté onion, ginger and garlic until translucent. Add broccoli and sauté for 2 to 3 minutes till tender and crisp. Add ground cloves, cinnamon, cardamom and mix well. Cool slightly and mix with yogurt. Add tadka (optional), cover and refrigerate. Serve cold.

Tadka (optional)

Heat oil in a small skillet. Add cloves and sauté for 30 seconds. Add to broccoli mixture.

Variation

1 cup frozen spinach, thawed and lightly squeezed can be substituted for broccoli.

Cucumber Raita

2 cups plain yogurt, whisked
2 teaspoons salt
1 large cucumber, grated (gently squeeze some juice out)
1 tablespoon onion, finely diced
1 tablespoon tomato, seeded and finely diced
1 tablespoon cilantro, finely chopped
1 teaspoon roasted cumin powder
½ teaspoon black pepper, freshly ground
½ teaspoon cayenne pepper

Mix above ingredients in a serving bowl. Garnish with a sprig of mint and keep in the refrigerator until ready to serve.

Mint Raita

Omit cucumber, tomato, cilantro and cayenne pepper. To the yogurt add salt, onion, cumin, black pepper and 2 tablespoons finely chopped mint. Proceed as above.

Baingan Raita (Eggplant Raita)

Raita is a combination of vegetables or fruits with spices in plain yogurt. It can also be used as a dip or sauce. Traditionally, it is served with all meals.

This raita is similar to the Middle Eastern dip Baba Ghanouj.

1 eggplant, steamed, boiled or microwaved
2 cups plain yogurt, whisked
½ serrano pepper, finely chopped
1 teaspoon salt
1 teaspoon cilantro, finely chopped
For Tadka (optional)
2 teaspoons vegetable oil
¼ teaspoon mustard seeds
5-6 kari leaves

Cool and peel the eggplant. Blend eggplant and yogurt in a blender or food processor to a coarse consistency. Add Serrano pepper, salt and cilantro. Add tadka (optional)

Tadka

Heat oil in a small skillet over moderate heat. Add mustard seeds. When they begin to pop, add kari leaves and sauté for a few seconds. Pour over eggplant and mix. Serve cold with parathas or rice.

To use this recipe as a dip, decrease the amount of yogurt to 1 cup and serve with pita bread.

Gajar ka Halwa (Carrot Halwa)

Sweets and Desserts

Badam Burfi (Almond Fudge)

A burfi is a dessert, that is cooked to a fudge like consistency and cut into small diamond or square shapes. The thickness may vary from ¼ to 1 inch. It is usually made with milk (khoya), sugar and fruits, vegetables or nuts. Cardamom is the most popular flavoring, but nutmeg is also used. Finely slivered almonds or pistachios are often used as a garnish. Cooking the mixture to the proper consistency so that it sets is important and the last few minutes before removing the mixture are crucial. If the burfi is too soft, cook it a few more minutes next time.

2 cups blanched and peeled almonds
1 cup heavy cream
½ stick (2 ounces) unsalted butter
1 cup sugar
2 tablespoons finely chopped almonds

Grind almonds in a food processor to a fine powder. Do not over-process, as the almonds will become oily.

In a heavy bottom 6-quart saucepan, bring the cream to a boil over medium-low heat. Add butter and sugar. Heat until the sugar melts. Add almonds and keep stirring until butter separates and the almond mixture forms a ball (about 15 to 20 minutes). Stirring with a flat edge spoon will prevent the mixture from sticking to the bottom. Butter two pieces of parchment paper. Place the almond mixture on one sheet, cover with the second piece. Roll out the paste to a 9x9 inch sheet, approximately ½ inch thick. Remove the top parchment paper and sprinkle with finely chopped almonds. Cool completely, then cut into 1-inch squares. This is a soft burfi. Can be stored in the refrigerator for up to 2 weeks in an airtight container or frozen for 2 months. Makes 36 pieces.

Almond Kulfi

Kulfi is an Indian ice cream that was traditionally made in 4 inch conical moulds and frozen with ice and salt in large clay pots. Freezing it in cake pans or an ice cream maker is much easier for a large crowd. Breaking of the ice crystals is essential to get a smooth consistency. This recipe has been a crowd pleaser on numerous occasions.

1 cup almonds, roasted and finely ground (can use any type of unsalted almonds)
1 pint (16 ounces) heavy or whipping cream
1 pint (16 ounces) half and half cream
1 (14-ounce) can sweetened condensed milk
1 teaspoon cardamom seeds, finely ground
¼ teaspoon kevda essence
Falooda, optional

In a saucepan, mix cream, half and half and almonds. Bring to boil on low heat and cook for five minutes, stirring often. The flavor improves if the cream mixture is boiled.

In a large mixing bowl, combine condensed milk and boiled cream mixture. Using a whisk, mix well. Cool. Add powdered cardamom and kevda and pour into an ice-cream maker. Freeze according to the manufacturer's directions. Alternatively, pour the mixture into a cake pan and freeze for 3-4 hours. Take the pan out and using a hand mixer, beat the ice cream to break ice crystals. Place the pan back in the freezer. Repeat process 3-4 times to get a smooth consistency. Store ice cream in a freezer proof container. Cut ice cream in squares and serve topped with chopped almonds and pistachios and falooda. Serves 8-10.

Falooda refers to freshly made thin noodles and is available in Indian grocery stores. Follow directions on the package.

Apple Nirvana

6 large apples, peeled, cored and cut into slices
¾ cup granulated sugar
2 – 4 tablespoons of butter
1 cup all purpose flour
¾ cup oats
1 cup brown sugar
¼ teaspoon salt
1 teaspoon vanilla extract
½ cup butter
1 cup large pecan pieces

Put apple slices in a well-buttered, 9"x13" pan and sprinkle with granulated sugar.

In a separate bowl, mix flour, oats, brown sugar, salt, and vanilla. Cut in butter until mixture is crumbly. Sprinkle over the apple slices and bake for one hour at 325ºF.

Remove from oven and sprinkle with pecan pieces. Bake for about 30 minutes more at 300ºF.

Serve warm or at room temperature by itself or with vanilla ice cream.

Can use 1 kind or a mixture of different varieties of apples. Use regular oatmeal or 1 minute oats. Do not use instant oats.

Caramel Custard

Caramel custard is a legacy of the British Raj in India. A very popular dessert, it is often served with western meals and is an integral part of a Parsi menu. In India, it is steamed in the pressure cooker .A fancy dessert with simple ingredients that are always available in the kitchen.

For Caramel
1 cup sugar
For Custard
2 eggs, well beaten
⅛ teaspoon salt
1 (14 ounce) can condensed milk
2 cups water
1 teaspoon vanilla
6 ounce custard cups, buttered

Melt sugar in heavy saucepan, stirring constantly. Pour into buttered cups.

Combine custard ingredients well and pour into cups. Bake in a water bath at 325°F for 45-50 minutes or until knife inserted in center comes out clean. Chill for several hours. Turn out on plates to serve. Garnish with berries. Serves 6.

Besan Burfi *(Chickpea Flour Fudge)*

1 pound (4 sticks unsalted butter)
4 cups chickpea flour (besan)
4 cups sugar
Seeds from 4 green cardamom pods
1 cup ground almonds

Melt butter to make ghee. Mix besan with ghee and cook in a heavy, open pot. Cook on medium heat for 5 minutes and on low heat for 15 to 20 minutes until golden brown and smell of roasted besan is released Stir constantly to prevent burning. Add powdered cardamom to the mix. After few minutes add ground almonds and mix well. Cook for 5 minutes. Add sugar and remove pot from heat. Let sugar melt and mix well. Line a wax paper on the back of a 10 x15-inch tray or a flat surface like the counter top. Pour besan mixture on it. Cover with another wax paper and roll into ½ inch thick rectangle. When cool, cut into 1-inch diamonds, squares or triangles. Besan burfi freezes well. Serves 20.

Badam Puri

3 cups almonds, powdered
1 cup sugar
¼ teaspoon saffron,
10 green cardamoms, peeled and powdered
Milk

Mix almonds, sugar, saffron and cardamoms. Use enough milk to make dough. Roll and cut in desired shapes. Arrange on cookie sheet and broil on both sides. Cool and serve.

Chum Chum

A favorite dessert from Kolkota (formerly Calcutta) in the eastern state of Bengal. This often-requested dessert is wonderful by itself or part of a dessert table for special occasions.

1 gallon whole milk
4 tablespoons lemon juice
4 cups sugar
12 cups water
½ teaspoon rose water
Crushed & unsalted pistachios to garnish

Heat milk in a heavy pan over medium heat to boiling point. Add lemon juice and mix well. Milk will split quickly into cheese and whey. Pour milk over a triple layer of cheesecloth to drain the whey.

Run cold water over the cheese, squeeze and press it very firmly to get most of the water out. Put a heavy weight over the cheese for about 15 minutes to drain the whey. When cool, mash it with the palm of your hand in an open mixing bowl until no hard pieces are felt (about 10 minutes). This will form a pliable dough. Do not over -knead. Boil water and sugar in an 8-quart stockpot, to make syrup for cooking chum chum. Make flat, round or oval shaped patties, about 2 inches in size and carefully drop them in the boiling sugar syrup. Cook uncovered for 15 minutes on high heat and then about 10 minutes on medium heat. The balls will become spongy and rise to the top. Remove from heat and cool to room temperature.. Add rose water when the syrup is cool. Chill. Prior to serving drain chum chums. Garnish with crushed pistachio nuts and serve. Store covered in the refrigerator. Makes 48 chum chums.

Instant Ras Malai

1 can purchased Rasogollas
1 milk Mard Rabdi

Squeeze the syrup out of the rasogollas and soak them in Milk Maid Rabdi (available at Indian grocery stores) made according to directions. Canned rasogollas should be washed with cold water to remove excess sugar. Garnish with finely chopped pistachios.

Rasogollas

Make ¾ inch small balls. Roll in the palms of your hand so the surface is smooth. Follow the same procedure as cooking chum chum.

Chum Chum has been successfully made time and again. If you like rasogolla or chum chum this recipe is worth mastering with a little practice. The consistency of the cheese or chenna is very important. If it is too dry, the balls become hard and if too moist then either small flecks will come off during the boiling process or the ball may disintegrate. A good rasogolla is light and spongy and retains its round shape. Very dilute syrup ensures that the dessert does not become too sweet with prolonged cooking Make rasogolla or chum chum 1 day prior to serving as it takes time to cool and soak the syrup, However traditionalists in Kolkota do not like to refrigerate rasogollas as they become firm.

Gulab Jamun

2 cups original Bisquick mix
4 cups powdered milk
1 stick (4 ounces) unsalted butter, melted
1 (12 ounce) can evaporated milk
Oil for deep frying

Syrup

5 cups sugar
5 cups water
1 teaspoon rose (gulab) water
1 teaspoon cardamom
4-5 stems saffron or 1 tablespoon rum or amaretto

Mix the biscuit mix, powdered milk and shortening well by hand.

Add evaporated milk a little at a time to make dough. Dough must be pliable and must not stick to hands when rolled. Roll into tight balls about ¾ inch in diameter. Heat oil to 300°F. Deep fry on medium heat until balls are dark brown. Adjust heat as necessary. Remove from paper towel and cool to room temperature.

Syrup

Boil water and sugar for 5 to 7 minutes in a large wide pan. Immerse fried balls in the syrup, do not overcrowd. They will swell in syrup. Add rose water, cardamom, saffron, rum or amaretto. Turn off heat, cover the pan and let cool to room temperature. Gulab jamuns may be served warm, on room temperature or chilled. Makes 60.

Dudhi Halwa *(Cucuzza Halwa)*

1 pound dudhi (cucuzza squash), peeled and shredded
2 tablespoons ghee (clarified butter)
1 (15-ounce) container part skim ricotta cheese
4 cups Carnation milk powder
1 ½ cups sugar
1 (12-ounce) can evaporated milk
10 cardamom pods, seeds removed and crushed
10 almonds, coarsely chopped
1 teaspoon rose water
2 drops green food coloring

Squeeze the cucuzza to remove water and fry in clarified butter for 5-10 minutes.

Add evaporated milk. Cook for 10 minutes, stirring occasionally. Add ricotta cheese, milk powder, sugar, crushed cardamom seeds, almonds and rose water. Stir constantly until butter begins to separate from the mixture. Cool overnight or for several hours. Make 30 -35 balls and flatten slightly. Decorate with one piece of pistachio on top and store in refrigerator.

Gajjar Di Kheer *(Carrot Pudding)*

1 cup rice
1 gallon whole milk
1 cup carrots, grated
1 ½ cups sugar
½ cup golden raisins
1 teaspoon green cardamom seeds(ilaichi)
1 teaspoon almond extract
½ cup slivered almonds, divided, save half for garnish
¼ cup pistachio nuts, slivered

In a heavy pan, bring milk to boil & add rice and carrots. Cook on medium heat for 1 ½ hours until rice is thoroughly cooked and kheer has thickened. Stir frequently with a flat face spatula to prevent sticking. Add sugar, raisins, almonds, and cardamom (ilachi) seeds. Continue to cook for another 10 minutes. Add almond extract, remove from heat and chill until cold (several hours in the refrigerator). Garnish individual servings with almonds and pistachios. Serves 20.

Gajar ka Halwa (Carrot Halwa)

A popular dessert served during winters in India when ruby red carrots are in season. Addition of nuts and butter and serving it warm helps to combat cold weather in the north. This recipe for gajar halwa can be completed in only 30 minutes.

Halwa
2 pounds carrots, peeled and grated or chopped
1 stick (4 ounces) unsalted butter
1 teaspoon cardamom seeds

Sugar syrup
1½ cups g granulated ranulated sugar
¼ cup water
2 drops red food coloring

Paneer
1 cup Paneer from ½ gallon whole milk
½ cup powdered sugar

Topping
¼ cup slivered almonds

Heat a 4-quart heavy bottomed saucepan and add butter and cardamom seeds. Melt butter and add carrots. Cook on high heat and coat carrots with butter. Lower heat to medium and cover with a lid. Cook carrots for 10 minutes.

Add sugar syrup to carrots and continue cooking on low to medium heat, stirring frequently. Stir half of the crumbled sweetened paneer into the carrot mixture. Cook carrots to dryness. Spread halwa in an 8x8 inch pan. Top with remaining paneer and almonds. Serve warm or cold. The dessert can be molded and served. Refrigerate up to 1 week in an airtight container. Can be frozen. Serves 8.

Sugar Syrup

In a small saucepan, add water and sugar. Bring to boil and cook syrup to a softball consistency. Remove from heat and add food coloring.

Paneer see page 222

Gurudwara Prashad

This dish is traditionally served in Gurudwaras and is known as Pancham Karah Prasad (five ingredient Prasad). The fifth ingredient is the divine blessing.

½ cup whole-wheat flour
1 stick (4 ounces) unsalted butter
1½ cups water
½ cup plus 1 tablespoon sugar

Make syrup with sugar and water. Keep it hot. Melt butter in a skillet, add flour and roast on medium heat, taking care not to burn the flour. Stir constantly until flour is caramel colored and aroma fills the room. When the butter has separated from the flour, add the syrup. Stir to mix and evaporate all the liquid. Again when the butter is released the halwa is ready.

It is very important to stir constantly and waiting for the melted butter to be released.

Kaju Katli

1 ¼ cups sugar
½ cup water
1/3 stick unsalted butter
2 cups raw cashew nuts (kaju), powdered
1 cup milk powder
1 teaspoon cardamom powder
2-3 drops of rose water

Mix sugar and water, bring to a boil and make a syrup of 1 ½ thread consistency. It will take about 5 minutes of rapid boiling. Place butter and cashews in a skillet, cook over low heat for about 5 minutes, add milk powder, stirring constantly. Add sugar syrup and mix thoroughly. Cook till the mixture forms a ball and separates from the sides of the pan. Remove from heat. Sprinkle cardamom powder and rose water. Spread on an oiled wax paper. Place another sheet of oiled wax paper on top, oiled side down. Roll out to ½ inch thick rectangle. Remove wax paper and cool completely. Cut into 1-inch diamonds or squares. Can be stored in an airtight container in the refrigerator for up to a week.

Khajoor- Anjeer ke Ladoo (Date and Fig Balls)

¼ pound (1stick) butter
¾ cup sugar
2 ½ cups rice-crispies cereal
½ cup dried dates, finely chopped
¼ cup dried figs, finely chopped
¼ cup pecans, crushed
1 cup sugar powder

Melt butter on medium heat in a pan and add sugar. When sugar melts and begins to bubble, add rice crispies, dried fruit and nuts. When mixture is cool enough to handle, make walnut size balls and roll in powder sugar. Store in an airtight container when absolutely cool.

Karva Chauth Sandesh

This special treat is enjoyed by women in North India to break the annual Karva Chauth fast. Karva Chauth is observed by married women to pray for blessings and divine favors for their husbands. They dress up in their bridal best, adore their hands with henna and abstain from housework. It is an all-day fast, starting at dawn before the setting of morning stars and ending with the first glimpse of the fourth waning moon in October.

Chenna prepared from 1 gallon whole cream milk
¾ cup sugar
¾ cup milk powder
2 tablespoons unsalted butter
¼ teaspoon ground cardamom
¼ cup coarsely ground almonds
1 tablespoon sliced almonds or pistachios for garnish

Knead chenna, sugar and dry milk powder till soft and creamy or in a food processor with a plastic blade. The mixture should just become soft and not a paste.

Melt butter in a wok; swirl it around. On medium heat cook chenna, stirring frequently until it forms a lump. If it becomes too crumbly, add 1 tablespoon of milk. Add cardamom and almonds. Mix well and place chenna in a greased tray. Flatten it to ½ inch thickness.

Sprinkle with sliced pistachios or almonds. Sandesh is soft in consistency. Keep refrigerated until time to serve. Cut in a 1 ½ -inch diamonds when set.

Variations

1. Use ¼ cup chopped pistachios and a few drops pistachio flavoring instead of almonds and cardamom.

2. Tint 1/3 of the cooked chenna with yellow color or saffron. Divide in 10 balls. Divide the remaining white chenna in 10 larger portions. Place yellow balls inside the white portions, forming a smooth ball. Cut in half with a sharp knife and sprinkle with chopped nuts.

Chenna see page 222

Gajjarela Kapurthala

A very popular winter mithayee (sweet) when both milk and carrots are in abundance. Mehega Ram halvayee sat in a small 10' x 10' corner shop in Sadar Bazzaar, Kapurthala with customers lined up either to be seated for a hot cup of tea with Gajjar Pak or to pick up a carry out. In the mornings he sold yogurt set in an earthen pot, cut with a concave spatula to serve in a disposable fig-leaf bowl (doona) or whipped up a glass of sweet Lassi, flavored with Kewra (crocus oil). The air around the shop was irresistibly fragrant with Kewra. People had to stop. This is a modified version of Mehega Ram's secret recipe'; I have substituted condensed and powder milk for fresh Khoa, which is made by reducing fresh milk on low heat until it forms a ball.

2lbs. carrots
1 cup Sugar
½ can condensed milk (5 oz.)
2 cups dry powder milk
½ cup unsalted Butter
1 tsp. green cardamom, crushed
½ cup almonds, separated, crushed
¼ cup desiccated coconut

Topping layer
½ stick unsalted butter
14 oz. whole milk Ricotta cheese
1 cup sugar
1 cup powder milk
4 drops kewra
4 or 5 Silver waraks (Silver foil)
1 tablespoon (each) pistachio nuts and almonds, slivered

Wash, peel and grate carrots and place them in a buttered, stainless steel, heavy sauce pan. Sprinkle sugar on top in a uniform layer. Cook on medium heat for half an hour or so until the carrots are soft. Stir to mix sugar. Add condensed milk and continue to cook stirring frequently until the liquid evaporates. Add powder milk and cook for two minutes stirring constantly. Remove from heat and set aside.

In a clean wok, melt and heat butter until sizzling. Add cardamom then coconut and then almonds, about 3 seconds apart, give the mixture a quick stir and then add cooked carrot mix. Stir well to mix, Carrots should turn transparent and slightly darker in color.

Remove onto a lightly buttered cookie sheet. Pat down to make a firm layer, about ½ inch thick.

Topping

Melt butter in a heavy skillet, add ricotta cheese and cook on medium heat until smooth and color turns slightly. Add sugar and continue to cook on medium heat until sugar begins to bubble on the edges. Add powder milk and cook for 1 minute, stirring constantly. Remove from heat, add kewra, mix and immediately pour over the Gajjarella spread up in an even layer over the carrots' mixture. Garnish with warak, almonds and slivered pistachios. Cool and cut into 1 ½ inch squares. Serve with tea or as a dessert. May mold and serve in the middle of a dessert platter.

Low-fat Pineapple Delight

Burfis are traditionally made with khoya. Replacing khoya with part skim Ricotta Cheese and low fat milk powder not only reduces the calories but saves hours in making khoya. The use of Splenda also makes it a dieter's favorite.

2 (15-ounce) containers, part skim Ricotta Cheese
1 can (15- ounce) crushed pineapple in juice, drained well
1 cup milk powder
6 packets Splenda or ½ cup sugar
Preheat oven to 350°F

Spray a 13x9 inch glass pan or pie plate with non-stick cooking spray. Mix all ingredients in a large bowl and pour into the pan. Bake uncovered at 350°F. for about 1 hour. When cool, cut into 1 to 2-inch squares. Serves 12.

Maida Burfi *(White Flour Fudge)*

This recipe is dedicated to the memory of Mrs. Satya Jindia, a person, dear to many hearts in our commuity. She left many tastes behind!

1 ½ sticks unsalted butter
3 ½ cups powder milk
½ pint whipping cream
1 ¼ cups all-purpose plain flour (maida)
2 tablespoons Crisco shortening
1 ½ cups sugar
½ cup water

Melt butter, add whipping cream and powder milk and cook, stirring constantly for 3 minutes to make khoa. Fry plain flour in Crisco until light brown. Dissolve sugar in water and boil for 5 minutes to make syrup. Mix khoa, flour and syrup together. Spread in a platter to set, let cool and cut into squares or diamonds of desired size.

Mango Mousse

This is a simple, light, and elegant dessert. It is ideal for a summer luncheon or dinner as it can be made ahead of time and refrigerated. Using canned mango pulp makes it quick and easy to prepare. This pulp is made with India's finest mango, the Alphonso.

1 can (28-30–ounce) mango pulp
¾ cup sugar
½ pint (8-ounce) container heavy or whipping cream
2 cups boiling water
2 packets (½-ounce) Knox unflavored gelatin
Additional whipped cream and chopped pistachios to decorate

Combine mango pulp, sugar, and whipping cream in a blender in 2 batches. Soften gelatin in boiling water. Strain and add to mango pulp mixture and blend at medium speed for 1 to 2 minutes. Pour into individual serving bowls or a 9x13 inch glass pan. Refrigerate at least 4 hours or until set. Decorate with rosettes of whipped cream & chopped pistachios. Serves 8-10.

Gelatin may be softened in a little cold water first, then boiling water added, or it may be directly mixed with boiling water. Make sure no lumps remain. Although fresh mango pulp can be used, using canned pulp gives consistent results every time. It is available in Indian grocery stores.

Mishti Doi *(Caramel Yogurt)*

This is a rich, caramel flavored yogurt. Traditionally, in Bengal, it is made with gud or palm sugar. The new, date palm molasses (notun gud) available during winter have a special flavor. Traditionally, the milk is first boiled to thicken, then sweetened and set to make yogurt. This is a 1-step, easy to make, fool proof recipe.

1 cup plain yogurt
1 (14 ounce) can condensed milk
1 (12 ounce) can evaporated milk

In a medium bowl, whisk yogurt till smooth, add condensed milk and mix well. Add evaporated milk and blend well. Do not beat. Pour into an 8-inch square 1 ½ quart Pyrex pan and bake at 200° F for 1 ½ hours. Cool to room temperature and refrigerate for several hours before serving. Serve plain or with chilled segments of mandarin oranges and chopped pecans. Serves 8.

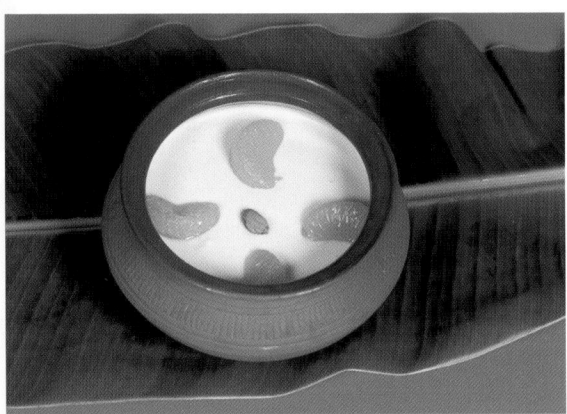

Puja Halva

1 cup Cream of Wheat
1 ½ sticks (6 ounces) unsalted butter
1 cup sugar
¼ cup chopped almonds
¼ cup dried pineapple, chopped
4 strands saffron (optional)
¼ teaspoon green cardamom seeds
3 cups milk
1 cup cream

Melt butter in a heavy 4-quart pan on low heat. Add cream of wheat and raise heat to medium. Roast the cream of wheat until golden brown. Reduce heat and add sugar, almonds, pineapple, saffron and cardamom seeds. Mix well. Add milk and cream, stir to dissolve the sugar and bring to a boil. Cover and simmer until all the milk has been absorbed and a bit of oil has separated from the cream of wheat. Stir often to prevent burning. Serve warm or cold. Serves 6-8.

Saffron Rice Kheer

Kheer is a milk pudding. Kheer can be made with rice, wheat, vermicelli sago, and vegetables such as cuccuza, carrots, and fruits like apples. Rice pudding is made in many countries but the flavoring of saffron and cardamom is unique to India. The pale yellow color of the saffron kheer with chopped green pistachios looks pretty.

2 quarts (32 ounces) milk, preferably whole milk
½ cup basmati rice, or any long grain rice
½ cup water
¾ cup sugar or to taste
¼ teaspoon saffron , plus 2 tablespoons milk
4 green cardamoms, peeled and seeds crushed or powdered
20 almonds, peeled and finely slivered or chopped
20 unsalted pistachios peeled and finely chopped

In a heavy bottomed saucepan, bring milk to a boil over medium heat, stirring occasionally to prevent from sticking to the bottom. Simmer on medium heat for 10 minutes. Meanwhile, wash rice and drain on a paper towel. Crush the rice coarsely in a food processor taking care not to turn it into a powder. Mix rice with cold water. Add slowly to the boiling milk, stirring constantly to prevent milk sticking to the bottom of the pan. Simmer for 15 to 20 minutes until thickened. Stir often to mix the film of cream that forms on top and scrape the bottom to prevent milk form sticking to the bottom of the pan. When nearly done the rice grains will be uniformly distributed in the milk .Add sugar and stir. Meanwhile, warm 2 tablespoons of milk in a small bowl. Crush or powder saffron threads and add to the warm milk. Let steep for 5 minutes, so as to allow the color & flavor to develop. Add to the rice-milk mixture. Add half the of almonds and pistachios. Keep the remaining for garnishing. Simmer the mixture for 5 minutes. Remove pan from heat and cool to room temperature. Refrigerate until serving time. Serve cold in small bowls and garnish with almonds and pistachios.

The consistency of kheer can be thick or thin. It is usually not as thick as American rice pudding. The consistency will depend on how long you boil the milk with the rice. It will thicken some more after being refrigerated. If it is too thick I sometimes add a few tablespoons of milk to change the consistency prior to serving.

Saffron Pistachio Ice Cream

This wonderful golden- colored ice cream is always a big hit during summer dinner parties. Served in sterling silver ice cream bowls, it is a fitting finale to a royal feast.

1 teaspoon saffron
1 tablespoon milk
3 pints (24 ounces) half and half
1 ½ pints (12 ounces) heavy or whipping cream
2 ¼ cups sugar
¼ cup finely ground pistachios and almonds, mixed
1 teaspoon cardamom seeds, finely ground
Toasted almonds and pistachios for garnish

Toast saffron in microwave for 15 seconds (be careful not to burn it) and crush in the palm of your hand. Heat milk, add crushed saffron and let it steep for 4-5 minutes.

In a cold mixing bowl, add half and half, cream and sugar. Mix well to dissolve the sugar. Add nuts, cardamom and saffron milk. Mix well and pour into an ice cream maker. Freeze according to manufacturer's directions. Alternatively, cover the bowl and place in the freezer for 3-4 hours. Take it out and using a mixer, mix the ice cream to break ice crystals. Place the bowl back in the freezer. Repeat the process for 3-4 times. Store ice cream in a freezer proof container. Serve the ice cream topped with toasted & crushed almonds and pistachios. Serves 8-10.

Sandesh

There are a number of varieties of sandesh and these are made with various flavors and with different textures. This recipe is easy and quick to make.

1 gallon whole milk
3 tablespoons lemon juice or vinegar
½ cup sugar
½ can condensed milk

Follow directions to make chenna (page 222). Let chenna cool to touch. Add sugar, mix and knead by hand or food processor. Do not over process. Place in a saucepan with heavy bottom & cook on medium heat. Stir constantly until mixture starts leaving the sides of the pan. Add condensed milk and cook for a few minutes, stirring constantly. Remove from heat. While still warm, divide into equal portions and make small balls (½ to 1inch). Press into molds to shape the balls. Balls can also be flattened and served. Sandesh will stay fresh for 7 days in the refrigerator.

Variations

Mango or Orange Sandesh

Take a ripe mango, peel and dice into small chunks. Scrape off the pulp from the seed. Add pulp to ½ of chenna after it has been cooked. Using a pie pan, layer the chenna-pulp mixture. Chill. Spread remaining chenna on top. Add mango pieces and garnish with whipped cream.

Oranges can be substituted for mangoes and a little yellow color can be added to differentiate the layers.

Sev Kheer *(Vermicilli Pudding)*

Kheer is a popular milk- based dessert in India. It is a simple dessert to make. Apples, carrots and lentils like mung dal and chana dal are also used in different parts of India. In South India, kheer is called payasam.

1 teaspoon ghee or oil
1 cup vermicelli sev
4 cups milk
1 (14-ounce) can condensed milk
½ teaspoon rose water
20 almonds (soaked and peeled)

Heat ghee in a pan, add vermicelli sev and sauté for one minute on medium heat until light brown. Keep aside. Boil the milk, add roasted vermicelli and cook for few minutes until vermicelli is mixed well and swollen. Add condensed milk and stir well. Add rosewater. Cool in the refrigerator. Serve chilled, garnished with peeled almonds. Serves 6

The vermicelli used here is a very thin variety available in Indian grocery stores. It comes plain as well as roasted. The consistency of kheer is usually on the runny side. Remember, kheer will thicken after it is refrigerated!

Shyam Gulab Jamuns

2 cups Carnation powder milk
1 cup self-rising flour
3/4 pint whipping cream
Oil to deep fry
Tablespoon, slivered
Pistachio nuts for garineshing
Syrup
2 cups sugar
2 cups water

Mix powder milk, self-rising flour and whipping cream to make soft and smooth dough, Roll into 1- inch balls. Fry in cooking oil at medium high heat to very dark brown. Cool on a layer of absorbent paper. Mix sugar and water in a wide pan and boil for five minutes to make syrup. Add cooled gulab jamuns to hot syrup and cover the pan. Simmer for twenty minutes. Allow gulab jamuns to remain in the syrup until cool. Remove from syrup and arrange in a serving platter. Garnish with warak and slivered pistachio nuts.

Shrikhand *(Yogurt Delight)*

This easy–to- make dessert comes from the western state of Gujarat, where it is served with puris as part of the main meal. Although not very high in calories, it has a very rich taste. Served in small quantities by itself, or with chopped fruits and a dessert cookie after a spicy meal.

6 cups plain yogurt
½ cup powdered sugar
¼ teaspoon powdered saffron or 5-6 strands of saffron
¼ teaspoon ground nutmeg, optional
¼ teaspoon ground cardamom
2-4 tablespoons unsalted pistachio nuts coarsely chopped

Hang yogurt in two layers of cheesecloth over a bowl to catch the drippings. Allow it to drain overnight or at least for 5 hours. Scrape drained yogurt into a bowl. It should be thick and half the original volume. Add powdered sugar and saffron to yogurt. Beat with a whisk. (If you are using saffron strands, soak them in a tablespoon of warm milk before adding to the drained yogurt.) Flavor Shrikhand with chopped pistachios, nutmeg and cardamom. Cover and chill thoroughly before serving.

The recipe can easily be doubled. Shrikhand freezes well.

Jalebi

For the Dough
2 cups all purpose flour
1 cup yogurt
3/4 packet yeast
1 tablespoon all -purpose flour

For the Syrup
2 cups sugar
1 cup water
1 teaspoon lemon juice
Vegetable oil to deep fry

Mix 2 cups flour, yogurt and yeast in a medium size bowl. Cover and keep over night in a warm, draft-free place.

Next morning, add 1 tablespoon plain flour and beat well to the consistency of pancake batter by adding a bit of water.

Prepare syrup: Mix sugar and water and bring to a boil while stirring. Boil to 1-string consistency, (about 2 rolling boils). Keep warm. Heat oil in a flat-bottom pan to 375⁰ F. Check the oil for proper temperature. When the dough comes to the surface instantly, it is ready. Put dough in a funnel (may use a ketchup bottle) with 1/8" opening. Pour jalebies in coil shapes in the oil in a single layer, turn once, fry to golden brown. Drain all excess oil in the frying pan. Place jalebies in the syrup in a single layer for about one minute, until syrup penetrates the Jalebies, which turn translucent.

Syrup is ready to receive the second batch. Remove from syrup and place in a serving platter.

Serve hot. Serves 12.

Vesan

1 ½ cup clarified butter (ghee)
4 cups chickpea flour (besan)

Syrup (Chasni)
2 ½ cups sugar
1 cup water
2-3 drops yellow food coloring

Melt butter and add besan. Cook on medium heat until golden brown for approximately 20 minutes.

Stir constantly to prevent burning.

Remove from heat and set aside to cool. Mix sugar, water and yellow color in a saucepan. Bring to a boil and simmer until the syrup reaches one thread consistency.

Cool the syrup a little and add to cooled besan. Stir and mix well and pour quickly into a 9" x 13"pan to set. Besan at this time looks thin and has an appearance of pancake batter. But after cooling, it thickens and firms up.

Garnish with slivered pistachio nuts. Cool & let it set for 1 hour. Cut into 1-2 inch squares. The finished product is silky and smooth in texture.

It is very important that besan is cooked thoroughly. Undercooked besan will taste unpleasant, and overcooked will taste burnt. Patience is required for cooking besan. This process is very similar to making a dark roux.

Glossary, Techniques and Thalis

Glossary

Spices are used as flavorings or condiments and are derived from seeds, leaves, bark and roots of the plant. They are essentially used for enhancing the taste of food. The very word "Spice" kindles the taste buds and brings pleasure to the mind. Ideally, whole spices are best - they may be used whole in a spice sachet and removed prior to serving. They may be ground, as needed, in a coffee grinder or in a mortar. Spices are best stored in airtight containers and kept in a cool dark place, preferably in a wooden cabinet.

The list below provides Indian names for ingredients:

All-Purpose Flour	Maida
Almond	Badam
Anise Seeds	Saunf
Asafetida	Hing
Bay Leaves	Tej Patta
Black Cardamom	Badi Ilaichi, Kali Ilaichi
Black Chickpeas	Kala Chana
Black Lentils, Black Gram	Urad Dal
Black Peppercorns	Kali Mirch, Kali Miri
Black-Eyed Peas	Lobhia
Cardamom	Ilaichi
Carrots	Gajjar
Cashew	Kaju
Cassia	Dalchini
Cayenne	Red Chili, Lal Mirchi
Chai Masala	A mixture & spices
Chickpea Flour	Besan
Chickpeas, Garbanzo Beans	Kabuli Chana
Chili, Red or Green	Mirch, Lal or Hari
Cinnamon	Dalchini
Citric Acid	Limbuphool
Clarified Butter	Ghee
Cloves	Lavang, Laung

Coconut	Nariyal
Coriander	Dhania
Cornmeal, Cornflour	Makki ka Atta
Cumin	Jeera
Dried Ginger	Sonth
Dried Peas	Matar
Edible Silver foil	Warak, Vark
Fennel seeds	Saunf
Fenugreek	Methi
Fritters	Pakoras
Garam Masala	A mixture of various spices
Ginger	Adrak
Gram, Bengal Gram	Chana Dal
Hot Green Chili Pepper	Hari Mirch, Mirchi
Kari Leaves, Curry Leaves, Sweet Neem	Meetha Neem
Indian Cream Cheese	Chenna, Paneer
Lemon	Neebu
Lentils	Sabut Masoor
Mace	Javitri
Masala	A combination of various spices.
Melon Seeds	Magaz
Mint	Pudhina
Moath	Matki
Mung Beans	Moong Dal
Mustard Seeds	Rai,Sarson
Nigella Seeds	Kalonji, Mangrella
Nutmeg	Jaiphal
Pappadam	Papad
Panch Phoran	A mixture of five spices

Pistachios	Pista
Pomegranate Seeds	Anardana
Poppy Seeds	Khus Khus
Pressed Rice, Flaked Rice	Poha
Puffed Rice	Mamra, Murmura
Raisins	Kishmish
Red Kidney Beans	Rajma, Rajmah
Red Lentils	Masoor dal
Rice	Chawal
Rice and meat/ vegetable preparation	Biryani
Rosewater	Gulabjal
Saffron	Kesar
Sago	Sabudana
Sassafras	
Screwpine	Kewda, Kevda
Semolina	Sooji
Sesame Seeds	Til
Tahini	Sesame Seed paste
Tamarind	Imli
Thymol Seeds, Carom seeds	Ajwain
Turmeric	Haldi
Vegetables	Sabzi, Subji, Bhaji
Vermicilli	Sev, Sevian
WholeWheat Flour	Atta, Chappati Flour
Yellow Lentils	Toor, Toovar, Arhar Dal
Yogurt	Dahi, Doi

Punjabi Masala

The wet masala used in North India or in Punjabi cuisine starts with a few basic ingredients. Many optional items are added to customize the masala for a particular dish. For gravies, additional liquid is added.

1 large onion
2-3 cloves garlic, peeled
1-inch piece of fresh ginger, peeled
1 hot green chili pepper (optional)
1 tomato, diced or ½ cup canned, diced tomatoes
1 teaspoon turmeric
1 teaspoon cayenne pepper
1 teaspoon coriander powder
1 teaspoon ground cumin
1 tablespoon yogurt
2-3 tablespoon oil

Using a food processor, chop garlic, ginger and pepper, add onion and pulverize to a medium chop. Heat oil in a saucepan, add ground paste, Sauté until onions are caramelized and oil starts to separate from the roasted pulp. Add dry powders and mix well. Stir constantly and add tomatoes. Cook for 4-5 minutes and mash the tomatoes down. Add yogurt. Let the mixture cook for 4-5 minutes. At this point the masala will be a paste. This masala can be used for gravies or dry curries. It can be frozen in 1- tablespoon portions to be used later in the preparation of many Punjabi foods.

Variations

Cumin seeds can be used in place of ground cumin. Paprika when used gives a beautiful red color to the dishes. Cinnamon, cloves, or nutmeg can be added in small quantities to bring more complex flavors together. Tomato puree can be used instead of chopped tomatoes. Mango powder or amchur is often added to add tartness to the dish. Some folks like to add a pinch of asafetida in hot oil before adding onion paste. Asafetida has a very strong flavor and hence should be used in very small quantities. Garam Masala is often added to the finished dish.

To make gravy for curries, add 2-3 cups of water and bring to a boil. Simmer for 5 minutes. Add browned meat or vegetables.

Paneer, Chenna (Indian Cream Cheese)

Paneer. the divine and coveted item of Indian cuisine

Foods in North India are prepared using dairy products. A serving of yogurt is an integral part of Indian lunch and dinner. Paneer is a source of protein as most of the Indian population is lacto vegetarian. Paneer is the Indian cheese made fresh from whole milk.

---

1 gallon whole milk
¼ cup lemon juice or white vinegar

In a 4-5-quart microwave safe bowl, heat milk for 20 minutes on full power. Add ¼ cup lemon juice or white vinegar. Mix, and let the mixture rest for 3-4 minutes.

The milk will curdle and whey would separate. Line 3-4 layers of cheesecloth in a big colander and carefully pour the hot mixture into the colander. Drain whey and rinse with fresh water. Squeeze out excess water. Drain on paper towels.

To make chenna, the curdled milk is mashed with hands until smooth. Set aside for cooking.

To make paneer cubes, shape the curdled lump into a block of 1-inch thickness. Cover with paper towels and place a weight on the curd. Let it rest for at least an hour. Cut the block into 1-inch cubes. At this stage, the paneer can be used either as it is, or fried. Use in Palak Paneer, Matar Paneer and Biryanis.

Unfried or fried, the paneer can be stored in the freezer for 3 months. It is also available in the freezer section of Indian grocery stores. Prior to use thaw in warm water.

How to make ghee (Clarified Butter)

Heat one pound of unsalted butter in a heavy-duty medium saucepan, over medium heat.

Boil it until milk solids settle down and clear ghee is on top. Strain after one hour and save in a jar. Can be kept at room temperature for several days, or refrigerated for longer use.

Tadka, Baghar, Chonk, Phodni

These words are used as nouns as well as verbs. **The tadka** refers to the hot oil and spice mixture, that is added on top, after the dish has been cooked, especially dals.

To **"give a tadka"** refers to putting this spiced oil mixture on top of a dish.

A tadka gives an extra burst of flavor with minimum amount of fat since it is added at the end, and the dish is not cooked with the oil and spices.

Method

Generally vegetable oil or ghee is heated in a small skillet or a 4 inch metal bowl with a long handle over moderately high heat. The spices are added to release the flavors into the oil along with some herbs.

The tadka varies in different parts of India. Certain combinations are more prevalent in certain regions

North: Hing, jeera, coriander.green chilies,fresh ginger, fresh garlic, sliced or chopped onion

South: Hing, mustard seeds, kari leaves, dried red chillies.

How to make Yogurt

4 cups milk
4 tablespoon yogurt starter

Heating milk in the microwave is much simpler than on the stovetop as it prevents the milk from sticking or getting burnt at the bottom. Cleanup is also easier! This recipe has been made using a 700 watts microwave oven; adjust the time to newer more powerful ones.

Pour 4 cups milk (skimmed or other) in a 10-cup (2 ½ quart) microwave safe ceramic or glass bowl. Microwave on high, for approximately 10 minutes. Cool the milk till lukewarm to touch. Add 1 tablespoon yogurt culture. This is yogurt from a previous batch. Home made yogurt culture produces a better yogurt while store bought yogurt will make a sticky yogurt. In winter, warm the oven and then place the bowl inside. Oven should be switched off. Leave undisturbed, overnight. Yogurt should be ready in the morning..

Boiling milk an extra couple of minutes after it initially starts boiling will result in a thicker yogurt. During the summer or if you have a gas oven with a pilot light, you do not need to warm the oven.

A Thali

A 'thali', literally means a meal served on a platter. In olden times, the thali was typically served on a silver platter. Today, the thali is served on a stainless steel platter. The items in a thali can be vegeterian or non vegeterian depending on family preferences. Selections are based on regional preferences.

Gujarati Thali

The four typical components of a Gujarati thali are Rotli (wheat bread), Shaak (vegetables), Daal (pulses) and Bhaat (rice). During weddings, festivals or on special occasions an endless procession of fresh vegetables cooked in aromatic spices, a variety of crisp, fried snacks or savories (farsan), sweetmeats and a variety of sweet and sour chutneys and pickles are served in a thali.

Punjabi Thali

It is common to use clarified butter for cooking punjabi foods. In a Punjabi vegeterian thali, one or two selections of vegetables [Saag (mustard greens), Bhindi (okra), Alu Gobi (cauliflower with potatoes), Alu Matar (potatoes and peas), Matar or Palak Paneer (peas or spinach paneer), Baingan Bhartha (eggplant)], cucumber raita or plain yogurt, Dal or Beans [Chole (garbanzo beans), Mung Dal, Moth, Dal Makhani, Kidney Beans], cilantro or mint chutney and mango or lemon pickle, and wheat breads such as Naan, Chapati, Parantha, Makki Roti, Tandoori Roti are served.

For a non vegetarian addition, Keema matar (Minced meat), Kofta (ground meatballs in curry), Chicken curry or Chicken Kababs are included. Punjabi meals are usually finished with a serving of fresh fruits.

South Indian Thali

South Indian Thali traditionally includes pickles, papadums, coconut chutney, idli, rasam, vegetables (spiced cabbage, eggplant, green beans upkari, thorans), plain rice, flavored rice (lemon, yogurt) sambhar, plain yogurt, and dessert such as jalebi. It may include meat preparation such as Chennai chicken, Shrimp and eggplant.

Acknowledgments

Saffron to Sassafras could not have been made possible without the unwavering dedication of the members of the cookbook committee of "Sharing Shores." The time and effort needed were more than anticipated. The committee, in turn, could not have completed the project without the understanding, the support and the willingness demonstrated by the spouses and their families throughout the two years spent on the project.

Very special thanks to the Honorable Kathleen Babineaux Blanco, the Governor of our beloved State of Louisiana, for sharing a family recipe to be included in this cookbook. We are also grateful to various individuals, organizations and members from both inside and outside the Baton Rouge area that gave us the much-needed financial support. In addition to monetary contributions, we were also blessed by significant contributions in kind. Special mention must be made of **Tanuja and Ashish Bhardwaj of California** for their generous donation.

On the local front, an anonymous donor, Meena and Sham Sachdev, Chandan and Naresh Sharma, and several others made significant donations to the project. Our heart-felt thanks also go to friends and supporters who sponsored various fund-raising activities at their businesses and their homes. Invaluable assistance was provided by Chef Philippe Parola, who sponsored fund-raising activities at his restaurant, Vasken Kaltakjian for fundraising guidance and Pami Taylor who hosted such an activity at her home in Mississippi, Dvijen Desai to prepare Jambalaya for the fundraiser. Special thanks also go to Amarjit Singh Nijjar and Sukhjit Singh Brar and Company for hosting a fundraiser through an evening of Indian music. Jay Patel of Jay's Photography volunteered countless hours shooting the photos, selecting and preparing them for presentation in the book. We acknowledge famous Louisiana Chef John Folse for sending recipes to include from "Encyclopedia of Cajun and Creole Cuisine (2004)." Larry Livaudais, Professor of Graphic Design in College of Art and Design at Louisiana State University made "Sharing Shores" a class project and provided a winning logo. Thank you, Professor Livaudais and Laura Fukuda for the winning design. Attorneys Ben F. Melanson and Drew M. Louviere generously volunteered their legal expertise while Frank Briganti and Jason Stell created the web design. Julie Badeaux, Kathy Feig, Mary Joseph, Amisha Sharma, and Ed White provided assistance with editing the recipe text. Tony Moudgil, Sadhana Gera and David Phillips volunteered their time whenever called upon. To all these, and many special friends who allowed us to come into their homes to learn from them the secrets of some of these heirloom recipes, we say a great big "Thank You!" Finally, we thank in advance, all those who support "Sharing Shores" community projects by purchasing this cookbook.

"Sharing Shores"

Donor List

We would like to thank our donors/sponsor without whom
this book would not have been possible.

Platinum

Mr. & Mrs. Ashish Bhardwaj

Gold

Anonymous

Mr. & Mrs. Sham Sachdev

Mr. & Mrs. Naresh Sharma

Silver

Mr. Jeff Benhard

Dr. & Mrs. Jay Jhunjhunwala

Mr. Vasken Kaltakjian

Dr. & Mrs. Harsant Singh Padda

Bronze

Mr. & Mrs. B. K. Agnihotri

Mr. & Mrs. Ravi Diwan

Mr. & Mrs. Ranjit Mugve

Dr. Pami Taylor

Corporate Sponsor

Entek Environmental Laboratories

List of Contributors

Aloo Dal Vada	Mala Jain
Chiken Tikka	Chandan Sharma
Handwa	Manjari Patel
Hummus	Pinki Diwan
Khandvi	Bhavna Desai
Masala Peanuts	Bhavna Desai
Muthia	Manjari Patel
Nawabi Chicken Tikka	Chandan Sharma
Pakoras	Meena Sachdev
Quick Dhokla	Ila Vora
Ragra Patties	Bhavna Desai
Seekh Kabab	Dvijen Desai
Steamed Shrimp	Kajal Beck
Turkey Kabab	Deepa Mehrotra
Bhakri	Jyoti Shah
Bhatura	Sumir Chehl
Chawal Ka Paratha	Anita Jhunjunwala
Dal Ka Paratha	Bhavna Desai
Jeera Shahi Pratha	Sumir Chehl
Makki Ki Roti	Sumir Chehl
Masala Dosa	Sheela Venugopal
Methi Shahi Pratha	Sumir Chehl
Multi Grain Poora/ Chilla	Kala Ramachandran Virk
Paratha	Anita Jhunjunwala
Poori	Anita Jhunjunwala
Roti	Anita Jhunjunwala
Spinach Poori	Anita Jhunjunwala
Spinach Roti	Anita Jhunjunwala
Tandori Roti	Anita Jhunjunwala
Tomato Poori	Anita Jhunjunwala
Aloo Tikki	Pinki Diwan
Alu Chhole	Sumir Chehl
Bhel	Bhavna Desai
Coconut Chutney	Shalini Yennemadi
Dahi Vada	Ila Vora
Fruit Chat	Pinki Diwan
Garlic Chutney	Bhavna Desai
Mithi / Date Chutney	Ila Vora
Pani Puri	Anita Jhunjunwala
Tomato Kaju Microwave Idli	Kala Ramachandran Virk
Vadas	Sheela Venugopal
Hot and Sweet Cranberry Chutney	Nisha Valsaraj

Mint Chutney	Sadhana Gera
Sweet and Sour Fruit Chutney	Poree Sengupta
Tomato Chutney	Nisha Valsaraj
Tomato Curry/Chutney	Anita Jhunjunwala
Zesty Cilantro Chutney	Pinki Diwan
Ammaji Garam Masala	Chandan Sharma
Garam Masala	Rajani Sinha
Karela and Bhindi Masala	Sumir Chehl
Cranberry and Green Chili Pickel	Anita Jhunjunwala
Mango Potli Achar	Nirmal Gujral
Pinapple Pickle	Anita Jhunjunwala
Broccoli Raita	Anita Jhunjunwala
Cucumber Raita	Sumir Chehl
Dahi Bangan Raita	Kiran Jhunjunwala
Mint Raita	Sumir Chehl
Cabbage Koshimber	Shailaja Desai
Cucumber Salad	Bhavna Desai
Mint Dressing	Sumir Chehl
Sonth (Ginger) Salad	Sumir Chehl
Tomato Cucumber Moong Bean Salad	Uma Srinivasan
Ankurit Moong	Anita Jhunjunwala
Channa Dal	Anita Jhunjunwala
Dal Makhani	Meena Sachdev
Dal Palak	Pinki Diwan
Khajoor Anjeer ke Ladoo	Sumir Chehl
Masoor Amti	Chandan Sharma
Rajmah	Rano Sharma
Sambhar	Anita Jhunjunwala
Sindhi Curry	Simi Jaisinghani
Sookha Urad	Meena Sachdev
Almond Kulfi	Deepa Mehrotra
Apple Nirvana	Julie Badeaux
Badam Burfi	Chandan Sharma
Badam Puri	Urmi Chokshi
Besan Burfi	Sudershan Kharey
Caramel Custard	Angie Patel
Chum Chum	Pinki Diwan
Death by Chocolate	Governor B. Blanco
Dudhi Halva	Aruna Sura
Gajjar di Kheer	Ranjit Kaur
Gajjar ka Halva	Meena Sachdev
Gajjarela	Sumir Chehl

229

230

Crab Curry	Shalini Yennemadi	Banaras Italian Eggplant	Sagaree Sengupta
Crab Masala	Seema Banerjee Ray	Batata Song	Shalini Yennemadi
Fish Curry	Rajni Sinha	Beans Upkari	Chandan Sharma
Macher Jhal	Ila Sarcar	Bharele Baingan - Aloo	Rekha Parikh
Sour Cream Shrimp	Kajal Beck	Bharwan Bhindi	Jyoti Shah
Mustard Fish	Ratna Banerjee	Bharwan Karela	Sumir Chehl
Royal Bengal Whole Fish	Poree Sengupta	Bharwan Tori	Sumir Chehl
Shrimp and Eggplant Curry	Usha Hemmadi	Broccoli or Spinach Thoran	Mary Joseph
Shrimp in Yogurt Sauce	Bela Sen	Eggplant and Onion Delight	Baljit Randhawa
Very Easy Fish Curry	Purnima Singh	Gobhi Musalam	Sumir Chehl
Almond Pecan Cookies	Swaraj Gupta	Green Beans Talasani	Chandan Sharma
Aloo Bhajia	Bhavna Desai	Hariyali Kofta	Ila Vora
Aloo Bonda	Bhavna Desai	Jeera Aloo Subzi	Sadhana Gera
Aloo Tikki Stuffed	Bhavna Desai	Kaddu Sabji	Parvati Sharma
Batata Poha	Usha More	Kadhai Paneer in Microwave	Nirmala Sachdev
Chakli	Radha Ramachandran	Masaledar Tofu	Pinki Diwan
Cheese Fingers	Sumir Chehl	Matar Paneer	Krishna Agnihotri
Chivda	Jyotsna Shah	Palak Aloo	Anita Jhunjunwala
Coconut Biscuits	Seema Banerjee Ray	Palak Paneer	Meena Sachdev
Coconut Burfi	Sumir Chehl	Panch-Mela ka Saag	Madhu Beriwal
Dahi Toast	Madhu Beriwal	Rasedar Saunf Aloo	Chandan Sharma
Mathian	Tej Kaur	Saffron Corn	Sejal Desai
Sev	Rano Sharma	Sookha Aloo	Nirmala Gujral
Shakkar Paare	Tej Kaur	Soy Aloo Matar	Meena Sachdev
Tea Biscuits	Arti Sachdev	Spiced Cabbage with Potatoes	Poree Sengupta
Upma	Upendra Reddy	Surson Ka Saag	Deepa Mehrotra
Achari Baingan Bhaji	Meena Sachdev	Tava Masala Sabji	Sumir Chehl
Baingan Bhurtha	Meena Sachdev	Tava Mushrooms	Nirmala Sachdev
Curried Kashmiri Green Apples	Naumi Kak		

The Tale of Saffron to Sassafras

Saffron to Sassafras developed from wandering thoughts and abstract visions of six like-minded women from diverse cultures of India. These gregarious women frequently met at parties, religious and community gatherings. They shared a desire to do something meaningful for the community and had an inner calling to leave a legacy to consign for posterity. They were also popular and admired gourmets. They arranged community-gatherings, benefit banquets and fundraisers, cooking contests, cooking classes etc.; serendipitously, but surely, spreading the Indian aroma and a taste of the Indian hospitality and goodwill. All of them had lived in Louisiana for a long time, 25-45 years, creating delicious fusions of Indian and Cajun or Creole ingredients and culinary techniques. Their gourmet creations and culinary skills were in demand among friends both, Indians and non-Indians alike. Soon, these women with vast business, professional, social and culinary experiences, joined hands to tell the tales of their culinary trail from motherland-to–homeland and write a cookbook. Each one contributed unique talents and resources, knowledge and skills, devoting innumerable hours to put this project in proper perspective and bring it to fruition.

To our naiveté enthusiasm, producing a cookbook appeared a simple and straightforward task. However, we were to soon discover the complexity of the mechanics of producing a cookbook. The tribulations of the path of this grandiose mission, though extremely educational, were challenging. They tested our endurance, patience and, at times, the very faith in our own ability to pursue our joint dream.

Prosecuting the mission demanded serious planning and strenuous work; e.g., searching and seeking of resources; forming a non-profit organization, launching a membership drive; fundraising; testing, computing and compiling of the recipes; preparations for photography and shooting & undertaking numerous other tasks and activities which required endless hours of diligent labor. It was all made possible with overwhelming cooperation and support from the members, the community, friends and families. Kudos to the team who dared to dream and pulled the project through. The book would be incomplete without a few words on some specific contributions made by individuals who spearheaded this project.

Chandan Sharma, a youthful, retired pediatrician with enormous patience and tenacity, energy and capacity for legwork and an unabashed skill of communicating, who initiated this project, researched, resourced and tirelessly networked and labored for its successful completion. She worked with an unparalleled passion and stamped her seal on almost every aspect of this project.

Pinki Diwan's association with the corporate and civic organizations as the Director of the Donor Corporate and Foundation Programs at LSU Foundation, was invaluable in route mapping. She linked with numerous relative organizations and fundamental resources, which helped us to form a non-profit organization and subsequent charting of our plan of action. She continuously steered the program punctually and proficiently and was never too busy for Sharing Shores even when her plate was overflowing with multiple commitments.

Meena Sachdev, a businesswoman and a professional scientist, experienced in corporate project planning and coordination, took the lead in formalization and incorporating of the organization and subsequent planning and coordination of the project. Her uncompromising honesty, devotion, consistently long hours and systematic pursuance, kept the project on course. She was the propelling force in all the fundraisers and kept the wheels moving through ebb and flow.

Anita Jhunjhunwala, with her quiet and assertive mannerism and managerial authority, made a difference in the practical phases of the development of this book. Being a past president of Hindu Vedic Society of Baton Rouge and Asian American Society of greater Baton Rouge, she was our vital link to the community.

Bhavna Desai, a dietician and a habitual winner of cooking contests, drafted her whole family, husband, sons and daughters-in-law, to hold Jambalaya fundraisers and technical assistance. Her willingness to do anything, anywhere, anytime and a contagious enthusiasm, was inspiring.

Sumir Chehl, a retired research scientist and a culinary hobbyist, with much involvement in humanitarian and civic organizations, provided subtle analytical guidance for rational and reasonable, directional focus. Her years of experience in teaching Indian cooking at LSU and creative ideas, channeled our culinary theme, shaped the non-recipe text and clearly characterized our mission. The name of the organization, 'The Sharing Shores' and that of the book, 'Saffron to Sassafras', were her distinct contributions.

Krishna Agnihotri, a widely traveled educator, with mature and broad perspective and international links, came in briefly like a magic wand and swept all the pieces together with the speed of a whirlwind. The lacking funds flowed in and printing was outsourced for cost effectiveness. Definite deadlines and an agenda to meet them were clearly charted. She provided the cohesion and momentum for completion of the book.

Though there were many discouraging moments, fortunately, there were no deterrents.

We work and cherish the strengthened bonds among us. We value the lasting friendships and the community relationships, which developed during the course of this project. We started with little, but with the providential blessings and grace, we have ended with a lot!

By Sumir Chehl

Index

Book Order Form

for additional copies of Saffron to Sassafras, or other order information

please contact
Sharing Shores Indian Women's Association, Inc.
(225) 753-1114
sharingshores@yahoo.com
www.sharingshores.org